Drugs in the family

Also available in this series

Random drug testing of schoolchildren: A shot in the arm or a shot in the foot for drug prevention?
Neil McKeganey

Exploring community responses to drugs
Michael Shiner, Betsy Thom and Susanne MacGregor with Dawn Gordon and Marianna Bayley

Parental drug and alcohol misuse: Resilience and transition among young people
Angus Bancroft, Sarah Wilson, Sarah Cunningham-Burley, Kathryn Backett-Milburn and Hugh Masters

Drug testing in the workplace: The Report of the Independent Inquiry into Drug Testing at Work
Independent Inquiry into Drug Testing at Work

Prescribing heroin: What is the evidence?
Gerry V. Stimson and Nicky Metrebian

A growing market: The domestic cultivation of cannabis
Mike Hough, Hamish Warburton, Bradley Few, Tiggey May, Lan-Ho Man, John Witton and Paul J. Turnbull

Times they are a-changing: Policing of cannabis
Tiggey May, Hamish Warburton, Paul J. Turnbull and Mike Hough

This publication can be provided in alternative formats, such as large print, Braille, audiotape and on disk. Please contact: Communications Department, Joseph Rowntree Foundation, The Homestead, 40 Water End, York YO30 6WP.
Tel: 01904 615905. Email: info@jrf.org.uk

Drugs in the family

The impact on parents and siblings

Marina Barnard

The **Joseph Rowntree Foundation** has supported this project as part of its programme of research and innovative development projects, which it hopes will be of value to policy makers, practitioners and service users. The facts presented and views expressed in this report are, however, those of the author and not necessarily those of the Foundation.

Joseph Rowntree Foundation
The Homestead
40 Water End
York YO30 6WP
Website: www.jrf.org.uk

First published 2005 by the Joseph Rowntree Foundation

ISBN 1 85935 319 3 (paperback)
ISBN 1 85935 320 7 (pdf: available at www.jrf.org.uk)

A CIP catalogue record for this report is available from the British Library.

Cover design by Adkins Design

Prepared and printed by:
York Publishing Services Ltd
64 Hallfield Road
Layerthorpe
York YO31 7ZQ
Tel: 01904 430033; Fax: 01904 430868; Website: www.yps-publishing.co.uk

Further copies of this report, or any other JRF publication, can be obtained either from the JRF website (www.jrf.org.uk/bookshop/) or from our distributor, York Publishing Services Ltd, at the above address.

Contents

Acknowledgements

My first, most heartfelt thanks go to the many people who allowed me to hear their often difficult stories. To speak to a near stranger about something so deeply personal and so affecting was a brave step. I have a different, but no less significant, debt of gratitude in particular to Professors Jim Macintosh and Neil McKeganey and also to the JRF advisory group so ably chaired by Charlie Lloyd. Throughout the life of this project they have offered constructive comment, support and encouragement. All were gratefully received. Thank you.

1 Introduction and methods

Introduction

It is a simple yet largely ignored truism that drug problems have a profound impact on families. Mothers and fathers, brothers and sisters are frequently caught in the maelstrom that drug problems almost inevitably create. If the effects on families have been ignored it is because of a preoccupation to perceive and treat drug problems as the preserve of the individual rather than having any wider ramifications for close relatives, and perhaps too an underlying assumption that often the family is the cause of the problem (Copello and Orford, 2002). The combined result of these positions has been to marginalise the families of problem drug users.

This report is about the ways in which problem drug use affects the family from the point of view of parents and siblings. It is about the difficulties that families confront in trying to respond to, and cope with, the changes that drug problems bring about for sons and daughters, brothers and sisters. Also, when drugs come into the family there is the danger that other siblings might become involved in problem drug use, further adding to family problems. Through interviews with problem drug users, parents and siblings, and also a small number of interviews with practitioners in the field, this research offers a small window into the devastating impact that problem drug use frequently has on families.

First it is worth looking briefly at what the research can tell us. The relatively small body of research can be subdivided into two: the effects that problem drug use has on the family, considered from the perspective of family members, most usually the mothers; and the risks of drug exposure and drug initiation between sibling groups.

Research on the impact of a drug-using family member on the family

This research has indicated the severe and enduring stress experienced by family members, which in parents can result in high levels of physical and psychological morbidity (Velleman *et al.*, 1993; Orford *et al.*, 1998). A recent government report on supporting families of drug users in Scotland identified four key areas of impact on relatives: physical and psychological health; finance and employment; social life; and family relationships (EIU, 2002). The playing out of problematic behaviours such as stealing, violence, argumentativeness and unpredictability in the home have all been identified as contributing to the difficulties of living with a family member who develops drug problems (Velleman *et al.*, 1993).

Even here, however, the focus has been on the impact on families from the perspective and experience of parents, most usually mothers. The impact of having a problem drug-using sibling on other brothers and sisters has been much less likely to attract research attention. Family therapists interested in treating problems within a relationship context have been those most likely to call attention to changed family dynamics and the roles siblings can come to adopt in relation to the drug-using family member (Huberty and Huberty, 1986).

Outside the field of drugs research there has been some consideration of the experiences of brothers or sisters living in families where their siblings have chronic illnesses such as cystic fibrosis (Bluebond-Langner, 1996), disability (Lamorey, 1999) or mental health problems (Gerace, 1993). As with siblings of problem drug users, these siblings considered that because their parents were so taken up with the care of their ailing sibling there was less time, attention and energy available to them. This was a source of some resentment and sadness for them too, although there was a greater sense of the pressing needs of the ill child.

Research on the transmission of drug problems to other siblings

The most prolific area of research on drugs and siblings, almost entirely North American, has considered the likelihood of exposure to and transmission of (problematic and other) drug use between siblings. Younger brothers or sisters of drug users have been identified as at increased risk of drug exposure and drug initiation. Boyd and Guthrie (1996) reported that 60 per cent ($n = 54$) of their sample of problem drug users had a sibling with a drug or alcohol problem. Similarly Luthar and colleagues (1993) reported that siblings of problem drug users were particularly vulnerable to developing problems with drugs, alcohol and antisocial personality disorders.

Researchers have pointed to the links between parental monitoring and control on a sibling's drug exposure and attitudes towards drug use (Hammersley *et al.*, 1997). The associations between family dysfunction (often including parental drug or alcohol problem use and childhood experiences of sexual or other abuse) have been observed in much previous research on the antecedents of problem drug use (Marcenko *et al.*, 2000). One can see the value of research to separate out the relative influence of a shared family history from an independent risk posed by an older sibling's drug use on the propensity for the younger one to try drugs. A very partial answer to this might be found in the work of Brook and colleagues (1989) on the relative influence of a drug-using parent, elder sibling and peers on the propensity for a younger brother to use drugs. This research indicated that older brother, parental and peer drug use each had an independent impact on a younger brother's drug use. However, the degree of influence from peers and older brothers who used drugs was greater than that of parents.

Duncan and colleagues (1996) have noted the significance of siblings in providing positive reinforcement for delinquent acts (this included drug use). As 'influential friends' (Vakalahi, 2001), older brothers or sisters can legitimate deviant behaviours by example (Jones and Jones, 2000) or coercion (through being goaded, for example) or through competitiveness. Needle and colleagues (1986) and Brook and colleagues (1983) pointed to the important connections between older sibling and peer substance use in predicting frequency of drug use through both imitation and reinforcement. Brook and colleagues report, for example, that 'older siblings and peer factors each had a direct effect on the younger sibling's stage of drug use' (1983, p. 88). The importance of this finding is precisely in the linkages between siblings, peer associations and the communities within which such behaviours take place. Being exposed to drugs through an elder sibling may not necessarily result in drug initiation. However, friends who are positively inclined towards drugs might additionally legitimate drug use.

Methods

The study aim was originally conceived in the narrow terms of the influence that a problem drug-using sibling might exert on the initiation of a brother or sister into drug use and how parents might respond to such a threat. However, it quickly became apparent that the answer to this research question was more deeply embedded in family functioning and specifically the ways in which families adapted in response to family members who developed drug problems.

This study took place in the Greater Glasgow area. Over a period of a year (2002–03) semi-structured interviews were carried out with problem drug users and, with consent, one or both parents as well as their siblings. Where possible, related family members were interviewed as this held the promise of a three-way perspective within the same family. In all, 64 interviews were carried out with:

- 24 problem drug users (referred to in the text as 'index siblings')
- 20 parents (18 out of 20 were mothers)
- 20 siblings (all younger than the index sibling).

It was possible to gather ten sets of 'triad' interviews with the index drug user, the sibling and the parent of the same family. The majority of the remaining interviews were between the index and the sibling or the sibling and the parent. In five cases, either it was not possible to obtain contact details from the index sibling for other family members or further contact by myself was unsuccessful. As three of these index siblings reported marked ongoing family problems which precluded further research contact it is therefore possible that the eventual sample of parents and siblings better represents more stable families.

Additionally ten interviews were carried out with practitioners whose area of work was either directly or indirectly concerned with problem drug users and their families. These included general practitioners, teachers, family support workers, social workers and drug treatment workers.[1]

The principal researcher carried out all the interviews. In most cases the initial contact with the index case drug users was through a local drug agency offering short-stay residential drug detoxification and methadone stabilisation. All of these respondents had severe heroin problems, although some reported concurrent problems with crack cocaine use. A small number of respondents were accessed through a family support group in Glasgow. With informed consent, confidential interviews were carried out that were tape-recorded and fully transcribed. All respondents' names and some details have been changed to preserve anonymity. At the conclusion of the interview research respondents were asked permission to approach family members. Participants were provided with a £10 voucher in recognition of their time. As it was only ever given at the very end of the research encounter and without prior introduction it could not be described as an incentive.

The interviews were analysed with the help of the software package NVivo. Themes were identified and fully explored through the use of deviant case analysis. This form of analysis involved the refinement of the model for explanation of phenomena by means of the deviant outlying cases. This worked on the assumption that a coherent explanation would have to account for all the cases without destabilising the overarching explanation for what appeared to be going on in these families. If it did not, then the overarching explanation could not be sufficiently robust, necessitating either its abandonment or refinement to include the outlying cases.

The next section proceeds by describing some salient characteristics of the problem drug users and their families interviewed for this study.

Describing the family

The mean age of the index case siblings was 23 (range 16–26). The majority of index drug-using siblings interviewed had a long-standing problem with drugs, usually heroin but probably best characterised as poly drug use. These drug problems had developed when they were in their mid-teens. With the exception of five index siblings the drug problem had developed while still living at home. One consequence of the longevity of the drug problem is that most families were long past the stage of discovering the drug problem and had adapted their responses to their drug-using child over many years. Inevitably this is reflected in the retrospective accounts provided to the researcher.

The following sections provide information on the index siblings' reported family composition and history, whether more than one sibling in the family or only one sibling had a drug problem. This forms an important backdrop to the subsequent discussion in Chapter 4 on exposure of siblings to drug use.

Families where more than one sibling has a drug problem

Ten of the index problem drug-using siblings reported that they had at least one brother or sister with a drug problem. Half of these came from large families with upwards of six siblings. These were all reconstituted families often with a number of different parents. Other research has also noted a clustering of problems with criminality and delinquency in large families (Farrington and Painter, 2004). In three families, multiple siblings (three or four) had developed serious drug problems. The birth mother and father had separated in three-quarters of the families where more than one sibling had a drug problem.

Most of the index siblings (seven out of ten) reported that one or both parents (or step-parents) had either current or previous problems with alcohol and/or drugs. Domestic violence seems to have formed the persistent backdrop of many of their lives. Five respondents reported being placed in out-of-home care for significant periods in their lives. One respondent reported sexual abuse by a stranger out of her home environment.

Of these ten index siblings, half reported that they had initiated the drug career of at least one of their other brothers or sisters. Of the remainder, it was peers who had been significant and in the last case, drug initiation was through her problem drug-using father.

Families where one sibling only has a drug problem

There were 14 families where no more than one of the sibling group had developed a drug problem. The most striking difference between these and the families where more than one had a drug problem was that, with the exception of one respondent, they did not come from large families. None of the remaining index siblings reported having any more than two other siblings. A high proportion reported coming from reconstituted families, with nine reporting their birth mother and father as having separated and a further two reporting having been raised by lone parents. Over half (eight out of 14) said that their mother or father or both had current or past problems with alcohol and/or drugs. Four of the 14 said that they and/or their siblings had been placed in out-of-home care during their childhoods. Again there were frequent reports of domestic violence and strife.

Four respondents reported being the victims of sexual abuse, in one case by a stranger out of the home; close family members had sexually abused the others.

Six of the index siblings reported knowing of some drug use by their other siblings but by their accounts it was not problematic.

The following chapter provides a detailed overview of the impact of a child's drug problem on families from the perspectives of parents and brothers and sisters.

2 The impact of problem drug use upon the family

It's like a living hell, a real living hell.
(Parent)

Introduction

The person who develops a problem with drugs is also someone's son or daughter and usually someone's brother or sister. Almost inevitably their problem becomes the family's problem. The purpose of this chapter is to delineate the ways in which a family member's drug problem affects family functioning and relationships seen from the perspective of parents and their other children. These relationships and indeed the whole tenor of family life are fundamentally affected by the development of the drug problem and the way in which it plays itself out over time. The most common response of families, at least in the early days, was to try to find a way to accommodate the problem whilst also seeking a solution to it. However, set against this was the near daily onslaught of problems brought about by trying to live in close proximity to someone with drug dependency issues. The family impulse to contain and solve the problem creates great stress, conflict and disturbance between family members, which are greatly compounded by the ongoing seemingly relentless negative impacts of the drug problem on the family. The effort to maintain some semblance of family life, to carry on regardless, was in all the cases here experienced as a near impossibility that could strain the family to breaking point. The chapter closes by showing how the strain over time of trying to contain the family member's drug problem whilst also attempting to maintain some family order and normality became too great for the majority of families in this sample, resulting in efforts to exclude the drug-using family member.

One father's experience

To illustrate the enormity of the impact of a family member's problem drug use and its capacity to affect every aspect of family life, this chapter begins by drawing on one father's account of the strains on family functioning and relationships once two of his four sons developed drug problems. The other families interviewed in this study confirmed and added to this picture of the family's struggle to come to terms with, and at some level adapt to, the drug problem and its complex effects on virtually every aspect of family life.

> *The wife was wantin' tae keep them in and I was wantin' tae fling them oot, ye know, and me and her wid end up arguing. She wid kinda stick up for them and I wid be slaughterin' them and sayin' naw they're no' ... ye know and things were steadily goin' missin' out the hoose and they other two boys were kinda saying ... know they were younger, they were sayin' tae me 'Da eh, ye know, I'm goin' this and this on Friday, could you come in', know, and I widnae come in of course and it wis fuckin' ... ye know they ... the younger ones, the two younger ones were good fitba' players an' all and wid say 'are ye comin' tae oor match on Sunday or Saturday afternoon?' and I wid say 'aye' an' of course I'd end up in the fuckin' pub and never went near them so I wis kinda neglectin' they two and stayin' out the*

other two's way and me and her wis like two strangers, ye know, tiptoeing about each other an' it just ... it just continued tae get worse ye know.
(Parent: Mick)

All of the elements of the family trauma are drawn here: the serious conflicts between parents as to how to respond to the problem, the father's withdrawal from the family situation and the mother's efforts to protect her two sons from further harm, as well as from their father, leading in turn to the degradation of their marital relationship and the diversion of parental care and attention from the other two sons. The clear impression is of a family reeling under the combined strains of the problems brought about by the drug-motivated behaviours of the two sons (for example, stealing from the family) and the jarring discordance of the parents' response to their children. As this father ends by saying, this was not the worst of it, in many senses it was just the beginning. In the ten years since his two sons developed drug problems there have been numerous bouts of prison, contraction of hepatitis C, episodes of overdose and more recently the development of mental health problems, all of which intimately involve the family.

All of the families interviewed for this study had passed the stage of discovering that their child had developed a drug problem. However, a theme running through their accounts of their response to the problem was the first and often sustained impulse to draw on the family resources to contain and resolve the problem. This is outlined in the following section.

Responding to the drug problem

Perhaps surprisingly, a significant minority (five out of 25) of problem drug users reported that their drug problem had gone undetected for a substantial period of time (the longest was two years).

R: ... so Amanda came an' stayed wi' me and that's when she wis pregnant wi' Sean and it wisnae really tae after she had Sean that I knew there wis somethin' no' right. See I didnae know she wis on drugs 'til then, d'ye know what I mean.

I: You had no idea?

R: No idea at all but then I knew ... 'cos ye know there's somethin' no' right ... she got paid her [social security] money on a Monday and wis comin' up and askin' me for a loan a money. And I couldnae fathom that oot. An' I wis goin' over tae see if everythin' wis alright, obviously the grandchild ye know, but I knew that somethin' wisnae right an' then it all came oot an' that wis eight year ago and it's been ongoing fae then.
(Parent: Mrs Sheen)

Families were almost universally thrown into disarray by the discovery that one (or more) of their children had developed a problem with drugs. It is hard to overstate the shock and profound dismay that characterised the parents' and siblings' descriptions of this discovery. For most, if not all, families it was an event of such deep significance that it completely and forever changed the family and its sense of itself. As this 19-year-old younger brother remarked:

Oh it's totally changed the family. It's no' a full family any more ... We all still love her. I do to bits. You don't treat her differently but in ma mind it's been spoiled ... the relationship. But back then there was good times when she wisnae on drugs that I can remember. Just you know, like a family that sat down eating together and all that. It was just a normal family.
(Sibling: Nick)

The drug problem in the preceding two cases had developed whilst the individual was not resident in the family home. Most families became aware that something was wrong before it became apparent that their child had a drug problem. Parents and siblings described the changed behaviour and appearance of their child sibling prior to the discovery of a drug problem. Cues such as being 'moaney' (bad-tempered), 'sleepy', having 'funny eyes' and always asking for money were noted as puzzling yet profound changes to their child. This brother commented on the changed behaviour of his sister when he was about 12 years old:

I: But you don't know how old you were when she first started using?

R: Naw she kept that quiet fae us. My ma and da found out because she wis always looking for money and stuff.

I: And did you notice things about her behaviour that were annoying?

R: Aye she wis always dead moanie, very moanie ... she looked dead depressed and that. I felt sorry for her when I seen her that way but it wis really annoying because she wis like always arguing about the least wee thing.
(Sibling: Andrew)

Commonly the family response upon discovery was utter confusion and panic, often in a context of a profound naivety about drugs and their effects and consequences. The impulse, at least initially, to contain the problem within the family and resolve it without recourse to external agencies meant that the only really likely port of call was the family GP but in most cases little help could be offered, particularly if the problem drug-using child did not want help in coming off drugs. Lacking knowledge and experience of drug dependency, the first reaction of most families was to prevent the child from accessing drugs in the simple belief that this would solve the problem. In some extreme cases this led parents to locking children in rooms to detoxify them. More than one parent or sibling responded with physical violence in the belief that this would be a lesson not to do it again. Such a course of action was never successful. At the start most family members had no real sense of just how intractable the drug problem was. It was in witnessing the extremes to which their child would go in order to get drugs that they began to understand the hold that drugs had over their children, as in the following example where even being locked in the top flat of a three-storey tenement was no deterrent:

She would smash up the room an' all this to get out. One time we said 'Right we're gonnae lock the front door.' We shouldnae need to do that. No mother should need to lock the front door on their kid but we were desperate ... And the next minute a lassie is shouting up 'Sonia, Sonia – Mary has fell fae the windae.' She had got to one up and had fell and she had cracked a bit of her spine. She wis in the hospital for about three or

four weeks and then she was in crutches for another three or four weeks. She was very lucky and I couldnae get how she was dying to get out. See this compulsion she had, she wanted out that door.
(Parent: Sonia)

In the face of this determination to get and use drugs, most parents attested to a sense of their impotence in both protecting their child and preventing the havoc that drugs were creating with their lives. This father described how his inability to alter either the course of his son's drug problem or prevent the dissolution of family life created in him an almost overwhelming sense of impotence and rage that further undermined the family.

Me and Shona [wife] *for ten year our life got kinda took away fae us, I felt that we were in a big hole, hangin' on tae the sides ... and I think it was the helpless, the powerless stuff, ye know, I was powerless. In ma whole life I wis never fuckin' powerless, I wis never powerless or helpless tae deal wi' anythin' that came ma way. One way or the other, I could deal wi' it but I couldnae deal wi' this, I couldnae change it, I couldnae make it better.*
(Parent: Mick)

The failure to prevent their child's drug use indicated to the family the significant place of drugs in their child's life and clearly signalled the gravity of the family's situation for the foreseeable future. This led families into trying to manage the situation. Frequently, however, the parents reported persistent and fundamental disagreement between them over how best to deal with their child. These disagreements contributed to the sense of family crisis.

I: So when drugs came in the family, that must've been difficult for you with your relationship with Joe?

R: Oh terrible, hell, because em his reaction tae it wis 'she's this, she's that' and it wis all the truth wit he wis sayin' but it wis the truth ah didnae need reminded a' every day and every five minutes a' the day ... Ye know, 'I hope ye know this and I hope ye know that' and 'she's just sayin' this' and 'she's' ... which ye dae know in yer ain mind, ye don't need somebody constantly tellin' ye.
(Parent: Martha)

Mothers were likely to emphasise their maternal responsibility to try to minimise the dangers associated with the drug use. In the early days at least, this seemed often to translate as a preference for keeping the child in the family home and out of harm's way. This can be heard in the following interview extract:

I think mother and ... you cannae break that bond. I mean other than that Sheena wouldnae be here 'tirely, you know what I mean? ... You wish you could cut, at times you wish you could ... sever that ... If that was a ... a neighbour, a friend, a cousin, an acquaintance, you could easily say 'oh, pfff, away you go, I don't want to see you again' but you cannae do that. As a mother, you cannae ... can't cut it, you know?
(Parent: Mrs Smart)

These mothers were aware of the costs to the family of pursuing this course of action but nonetheless saw their primary responsibility as helping the child most in need of it.

So Shane [partner] *says to me 'well, you're gonna have to sit and consider me, Dean and Donna* [other dependent children]'. *'Either that,' he says, 'or I'm off.' He went 'I've tried everything I can wi' them,' he says, 'you keep on letting them in and they're stealing'. I says 'well I cannae do anything else' I says, 'I'm still their mother and I'm no' gonna turn them away'.*
(Parent: Mrs Tavish)

It is important to bear in mind that all the interviews bar two were with the mothers. Fathers did not volunteer (nor were they volunteered) for interview, which greatly limits what can be said of their response to the problem. The interviews with mothers suggested that fathers were less likely to believe that keeping the child in the home offered much in the way of a solution. Such a view was perhaps more forcibly expressed by men who had taken on the role of step-parent; nonetheless birth fathers were also reportedly more inclined towards damage limitation through excluding the problem drug user from the family home. Mothers seemed to be involved in shielding the child from the father and vice versa. This was experienced as isolating and a cause of further conflict as inevitably their efforts were prone to discovery.

I think when you're a mother you know you say things and it's very hard to turn away. Very hard you know, to give up on her. I mean he just can't cope, can't cope with it at all ... And he's a family man, he's always just been for his family. And I tried to shield him from as much as I could, but with Lana [grandchild] and with the social workers and the panel he had to know because it had to come out. And he was quite taken aback when he heard all the things.
(Parent: Mrs Cairns)

What this amounted to was that parents, most usually mothers, were placed in the almost impossible position of trying to broker between protecting the drug-using child from some of the harms associated with problem drug use and protecting the rest of the family from some of the harms caused by the drug-using family member. This was itself a source of strain but so too was the often alluded-to sense of imbalance in the family as the negative effects of the drug problem permeated every aspect of family life.

The impact of the drug problem on the family and household functioning

This section considers some of the impacts of problem drug use on family members. These are considered under three headings: drugs as the focus of attention; theft and violence; and stress and anxiety. Clearly these are not discrete areas of family experience. However, it is a necessary fiction for the purposes of disentangling some of the ways in which a family member's drug problem impacts on the family.

Drugs as the focus of attention

The problem drug use of a close family member very clearly had a divisive impact on family relationships. The sense of all-encompassing family crisis had the effect of leaving other children somewhat ignored as attention was diverted to coping with the drug problem.

When she's on the drugs, she'd steal anything, everything aff ye if she could but also when she's no' on the drugs she's very demanding as well and Danielle's seen all this an' she must say tae herself, 'it's great, she's the drug addict, she's in there [drug rehab] *an' she's gettin' all the stuff'*

and Danielle's got tae work hard for everything she gets … I know where Danielle's comin' fae but at the end of the day I'm torn as well because yer just happy she's in there and she's no' got nuthin' so … I try tae juggle, ye know, likesay wi' Danielle, we went tae the pictures last week an' that wis an extra treat for her an' we had a good wee night. I'm the person that's tryin' tae keep three folk but I think unfortunate … I think the unfortunate scenario is that … oh I don't know how tae put it … oh I think Danielle could see herself as hard done tae, d'ye get what I mean?
(Parent: Mrs Sheen)

The mother in the following extract described how in trying to cope with her son (Paul) she had shielded him from the negative attentions of her two other sons. In her over-attention on Paul she had become estranged from her non-drug-using son Ade:

R: *… Ma son that stayed wi' me, Ade, he wisnae married, he finally walked … he went out the house … I kept sayin' tae Ade 'well you go because I'll need tae stay wi' him'. He wis mine, as if they wurnae mines* [laughs], *I mean that wis the stage I got tae, Paul wis mine, the rest could go tae hell.*

I: *How do you mean?*

R: *Well I didnae want anybody tae argue wi' him, I didnae want anybody tae touch him, I didnae want anybody tae talk tae him, he wis mine, I wis gonnae deal wi' the situation, but I couldnae deal wi' it.*
(Parent: Mrs McNabb)

The interviews with siblings tended to confirm this focal attention on the drug problem by parents. However, they differed in how they responded to this. The younger interviewees framed their response in terms of the need to give the drug-using sibling more attention, as in the following interview extract:

All the attention goes to him? It doesnae really bother me. 'Cos I'd rather the attention goes to him to try and get him aff it.
(Sibling: Dean)

The older interviewees were more reflective and did have a sense that they had been somewhat sidelined in all the focus on the drug-using sibling. The 18-year-old younger brother below was phlegmatic in acknowledging this:

… it wis just sometimes it wis just everything about ma sister and I wis just left aside a bit.
(Sibling: William)

This tendency for the needs of the family member with the drug problem to occupy centre stage was further exacerbated when their children became resident in their grandparents' home, whether temporarily or, as in four cases, permanently. A brother described the conflict of interest created by his sister and her son coming to detoxify from drugs in the family home just at the point he was about to sit important school examinations. His mother and father stressed that the family needed to all pull together for the sake of his sister but he resented the price it exacted on his academic performance:

I: *Yeah. I'm just thinking about that time, would you say you'd been close to your sister?*

R: *Well I've been as close as I can be just trying to help her through it and stuff like that. We just stuck together in the family and if Andrea was having problems wi'*

drugs then I would take Dan [his nephew] *up tae the room wi' me and stuff like that. When that was happening that was the time I was supposed to be studying for ma standard grades and it sort eh really affected ma standard grade effort because I didnae have the time to study. I still got all ma standard grades but no' as good as I could have done ... and I'm no' being selfish or anything but ma standard grades ... They were important to me. Back then because I was always looking after Dan because he was staying wi' us at the time, I just didnae get time to revise.*
(Sibling: Andrew)

In some cases the focus on the other sibling was not perceived as necessarily a bad thing since it allowed them to pursue their own agendas unimpeded, as this 19 year old remarked:

'Cause I've always seemed tae think that ma mum and dad and family are heavier on her, just because of wit she's done. Like anything she's done I've no' done. I couldnae think of anything that's bad whatsoever. Not ... I've done bad things obviously but the attention has always been on her. I'm no' unhappy about it ... It lets me get on wi' ma life. It suits me.
(Sibling: Nick)

Amongst these cases there were siblings who noted that their parents had not thought to ask how the drug problem had impacted on their lives. Again this is an illustration of the extent to which the problem drug user monopolises the family focus:

It wis ma mum that said tae me when she said that you were coming out. She said 'It never even dawned for me tae ask you how you felt about it.' And that wis six years ago, d'ye know wit I mean?
(Sibling: William)

A small number of siblings (three), including William above, reported that they were saddened and angered by the lack of attention they received and still struggled with the legacy of having been sidelined by their sibling's drug problem. This sibling remarked on the irony that the children who had not caused damage to the family should be the ones to miss out on their parents' attention.

But I do, I do love ma Ma and Da and I wid do anything' for them but wit can ye dae [laughs]. *I don't know, all I know is I wid hate tae be put in a position where I maybe had tae show, not more love but ... aye well tae me it seemed that they were gettin' all the love but I don't think they were. Is attention the word I'm lookin' for ... I don't know wit it is? They were gettin' all the ... everything, they were gettin', ye know, all the attention and everythin' wis Paul and Dan, ye know, and me and Nick wis, 'hey, we're here an' all, we're decent, we're good, we don't take drugs, we don't steal, we'll not steal out yer purse or steal yer fags or steal yer lighter or try and steal yer jewellery ... we're no' gonnae do anythin' like that'.*
(Sibling: Martin)

A striking feature of the interviews with siblings was their perception that their role was largely supportive or protective of the parent or more rarely of the drug-using sibling. It was unusual for them to refer to the problem as it played out in their own lives. In this sense the interviews were often more of a chronicling of the effect on the family than a detailed exploration of the ways in which it had directly affected their own lives.

Theft and violence

A major cause of problems for all the family members was the persistent theft of goods and money from the family home. This was a problem for all but five of the families interviewed. The scale of theft was stressful for all family members as it meant that nothing was safe whether the most mundane items such as toiletries and food in the freezer or more valuable items like jewellery. The following two interview extracts give some idea of the extent of the problem and the stress it caused other family members:

> *It wis terrible. 'Watch her there; she's away in the room.' I actually bought a double lock and put it on the room door and anything that was of real value ... I mean I was sitting one day and saying 'There's something different in this living room' and she stole ma big clock fae the mantelpiece. Do you know what ah mean? Everything went, all their games and all that. Bedding, curtains ...*
> (Parent: Sonia)

Brothers and sisters too reported that money and things of theirs went missing:

> *... There was a time I was going to Blackpool ... and I took all my money out. I was up and I got ready and all of my stuff was packed and ready to walk out the door and I went to get my money where I had hid it and it was gone! I was like ... and I'm in the car and all my friends are 'I'll give you money' ... I was like that, 'I can't go. So just go without me'. And I searched this whole town and I couldn't find him* [laughs] *but the time I did find him I had calmed down by then and I was like 'look, just stay out my face'.*
> (Sibling: Martina)

Those families who had children who stole from the home often saw themselves as under siege. The desperate need for money to pay for drugs was at one level understood but for families it meant a near constant request for money and a heightened state of vigilance to prevent theft from the home. As might be predicted, this greatly added to stress within the home as family members took on the task of surveillance:

> *Because when she's coming in and she's doing stuff, like trying to steal stuff and all that and it just makes your head just ... when you could be doing something else, it just makes your head really sore and you just feel knackered.*
> (Sibling: Danielle)

The refusal to provide money would often lead to angry disagreement that was both abusive and distressing. This can be heard in the following interview extract:

> *R:* *Like ... she'd start screaming at you, you know? For ... and calling you ... I mean she said some very horrible names, abusive things to you, that I couldn't believe they come oot her, you know? Things like 'I hope you die of cancer' and 'I hope you've got this, I hope you've got that' and if ...*
>
> *I:* *Why would she start doing that, saying all that?*
>
> *R:* *Just coming off the drugs and no' having the money to ... she'd want to borrow five pound off you, ten pound and you're saying*

no. Or she would appear – when she didnae live here she'd appear at the door, em ... 'I need ... gonnae let me in for five, ten minutes' and I'd let her in and then she'd 'can I get the bus fare, can I get this' and I said 'I'm no' giving you nothing' and then she would start, it was like horrible ... it wasnae even swearing at you, it was just horrible things that was coming out her mouth. Horrible things.
(Parent: Mrs Smart)

In at least one case the refusal to provide money precipitated violence on the part of the daughter with the drug problem when she was reported to have attacked her mother in order to get her purse. Her 13-year-old daughter ended up embroiled in the event:

R: *The worst thing would probably be when she gets violent 'cause ah can remember one time she was like just snoopin' around the house an' all that ... then she was like trying to steal ma Mum's bag for money and that. That was the worst time ... I wis mad, I wis just like pulling her and shouting at her an' all that.*

I: *Yeah. Were you scared that she might hurt you?*

R: *Uh-huh, aye, uh-huh, I thought ... I was scared.*
(Sibling: Danielle)

It was perhaps inevitable that family members reported becoming distrustful and suspicious in their contact with the drug-using child or sibling.

Uh-huh, uh-huh, it's always money, money, money. And I mean it makes me cringe when he puts his arm roon me and he'll say 'I love ye Ma' and I push him away because I know it's no' genuine ... And it's terrible to do that wi' ... but I cannae help it ... And that wis the reason I wis givin' him money, I couldnae cope wi' him because he kept on and on and on and on.
(Parent: Lena)

The lack of trust engendered by the stealing and the lying and the effort at manipulation greatly affected the family and strained parents and siblings alike.

Stress and anxiety

Many of the parents in this study considered that they had developed health conditions as a direct result of living with their child's drug problem. Reports of angina and stress-related health problems were common among parents who struggled with the many deceits and the constant arguments and who worried about the health and well-being of their children. Their lives were similarly afflicted by the unpredictability of their child's drug problem which meant never really knowing where their child was, the kind of trouble he or she might be in and whether the knock on their door would bring police or disgruntled neighbours or drug dealers looking to settle unpaid debts. The parent in the following excerpt felt overwhelmed by the damage her son was causing to her and the rest of the family, which in turn precipitated her decision to cease trying to cope with his drug use.

But em oh, it was causing just ructions everywhere because ... Like before I was always placid and like say it would be like 'what's for the dinner the night?' 'What do you think am are, a fucking skivvy? I'm no' running efter all yous and

I'm fed up daeing it ...' It was all just getting on top and then ... I mean naebody seemed to be bothering with the fact, you know what I mean, that ... I had found out that I had angina. That's what was making me feel no' well, and then I was having to get tests done and ... I've never had anything the matter wi' me in my life, you know what I mean, so I mean naebody as much as even asked me what was going through ma mind? You know what I mean? It's aw wee things like that and I thought well, 'fuck the lot o' them', you know what I mean? So that's just the way it's gonna be but as I say, if, if he's drug-free, fine. But if he wants to be on drugs he'll no' be here. He'll need to get his ain place because it's no' gonna work wi' him here.
(Parent: Mrs Smith)

Parents spoke about trying to shield their younger children from some of the negative effects of the drug problem but acknowledged that this was difficult to sustain as in the following excerpt:

She hasn't seen a great deal to be honest. She's seen it this year, aye. This is where all the explosives have been, you know what I mean, the arguments, em the carry on wi' this Liz and the carry on wi' them being charged wi' hitting this wee boy and she knows aw that. Like before she was never telt anything. Everything was kind o' hid fae her ...
(Parent: Mrs Smith)

For most siblings, however, there was little chance of avoiding conflict that permeated the whole fabric of daily life and indeed frequently spilled over into the public arena. Predictably this was a source of both shame and embarrassment for parents and siblings alike who then had to field the derision or pity of neighbours.

I: Is it shameful for you?

R: It is, they do because some of the times she's went in and she's stole other people's kids' toys and they come up and say 'She stole out the house'. And you go out and you feel it, you see the heads going and mibbae you'll walk up and they're goin' on 'Aw see these f'ing junkies. The bane of oor life'. And you're standing behind the person who's doing all the talking and the other one's trying to go ... You know they're trying to say 'His mother's standing there'.
(Parent: Rose)

In the same way that parents tried to shield their other children from the drug problem so these children also felt a responsibility to protect their parents. Although greatly upset by the experience of having a sibling with a drug problem they did not see themselves as responsible in the same way that their parents were. It was more likely that they would refer to the turmoil created in the house as a source of stress. This led to them intervening in arguments and on occasion trying to act as a buffer between their drug-using sibling and the parent.

Excluding the drug user

All of the families interviewed in this study had eventually come to the decision, often after many years, that they could not, after all, solve the problems of their drug-using child. Furthermore they also reached the conclusion that living in such close proximity to them was destructive to the family. Parents spoke, quite literally, of making a choice about the family's survival. The decision to try to contain the damage, most usually by the institution of rules limiting access to the house and family members, was arrived at with great difficulty. Parents were greatly burdened by the sense of having rejected their child, by anxiety that their child would be exposed to harm and by the inescapable sense of having failed as a parent. In the following interview extract this mother describes the point where she could no longer sustain the destruction of the family home.

> *So he come up ... and I eventually let him in and he'd stole Dean's chain wi' the RFC, it was his pride and joy. And that was the last straw. So he come up the next night wi' Anna* [his girlfriend] *... He come up to me and the rain was stoating* [pouring], *and I mean absolutely stoating. He come up to me about quarter to one in the morning, chapped us up out our beds ... I open the door and he just goes to come in. I went 'you're no' coming in'. Anna is about four months pregnant ... I went 'you're not getting back in this house again'. I says 'I've got Donna and Dean'* [younger children], *I says, 'these two their nerves are shattered' I says 'for the age o' them'... And that was my turning point with Richard; see when I sent him away? .... When I went to the window the rain was stoating ... Shane* [partner] *... he starts getting ready and gets his boots and he went 'I'm going to get him'. Because of the state I was in, because I turned him away, and I went 'don't – just leave him, leave him' and that's when I sort of I gained respect from Richard.*
> (Parent: Mrs Tavish)

When parents reached the point where they considered they could no longer live with the effects of the drug problem on the household they typically set in place rules of engagement with their child. Most usually these were that the child with the drug problem was welcome in the house only when they were drug free; that they were not to use drugs in the house; that they were not going to be given any money; and that contact with brothers and sisters would be dependent upon not being under the influence of drugs. Although the institution of such rules represented a significant turning point for most families it is important to note that these were not immutable. First, problem drug use is characterised by phases of relapse and recovery so contact with the family was apt to increase and decrease through the changing patterns of drug usage. Second, life events would bring families back together. For example, pregnancy on the part of a problem drug-using daughter could lead to her moving back into the family home. Third, there was no necessary reason to suppose that the rules instituted by the family would be adhered to by the child with the drug problem. The following interview extract is an example of what might be an unusually persistent son but it does nonetheless demonstrate a certain sense of the permeability of such 'rules'.

> *Aye but I'm a prisoner in ma own house, I'm frightened tae go oot in case he appears because he would knock ma door in tae get in, I mean he's done it. Three o' them it took tae pull him away from ma door. One day he wis determined he wis gettin' in and I wis tryin' tae hold the door shut.*
> (Parent: Lena)

One of the very difficult aspects for families withdrawing protection and support from the child with the drug problem was their greater vulnerability to danger. Almost universal mention was made of the fear of the knock on the door to confirm the families' worst fears. Fatal overdose is not unusual among problem drug users (Neale, 2002) nor is injury or even death through drug-related violence. Parents spoke of the double-edged sword of the relative peace in the household but at the cost of an unceasing anxiety as to its provenance:

> *... And it's strange because when they're no' here, you can get on wi' it a wee bit better but you're still ... you never let your guard down. But you know what's coming each day. But you don't hear fae them and ye put on the radio and ... there's a body of a young woman found or whatever. Or if you see a police car coming you automatically think they're coming to your door or ... It's them, you don't know where they are. You're getting peace because you're no' having the verbal and the confrontations you have with them and everything else. But you've still got that worry, it's still there, it never goes away. 'Where are they? What are they doing?' If you don't hear from them within three month 'Are they still alive?'*
> (Parent: Rose)

Limiting the extent and nature of the drug-using child's contact with the family did, however, benefit family dynamics. Parents and siblings reported that the house was calmer; there was less tension and fewer ructions.

> I: *Yeah. And has it got better for you now?*
>
> R: *I'd say it's calmed doon a bit 'cos I'm used to, it's like I'm no' used to seeing them as much as now, it's calmed right, calmed right doon. It's good for ... I'm glad that Richard is away a while getting off it.*
> (Sibling: Dean)

With the exclusion of the drug user, the household was less unpredictable and volatile, which allowed family members some ability to relax their guard in a more stable and routinised environment than had previously been possible. Furthermore there was some indication from the interviews that the exclusion of the drug user marked a watershed as some parents thought this had been a spur to their drug-using child's efforts to recover from drugs.

Conclusion

The impact that a family member's drug use has on the whole family and every aspect of family life is profound. The general impulse to manage and contain the problem was almost always found to create more problems than it solved and most usually led families to the distressing position of having to exclude the drug user whether temporarily or permanently. The commonality of the themes of family distress, confusion, anger, impotence and dysfunction in the face of the problems created by the child's drug use as well as the dynamic from the initial reaction to exclusion suggest the importance of initiatives to help families to come to terms with and respond to their child's drug problem and its effects on them.

The next chapter moves from consideration of how the drug problem affected the way the family operated to a concern with the ways in which siblings felt their brother's or sister's drug problem had affected them in particular.

3 The impact of sibling drug use upon younger siblings

Introduction

This chapter looks specifically at the impact on brothers and sisters of the drug problems of their older siblings. The different roles and responsibilities of parents and children mediated the ways in which they responded to the drug problem. Parents generally considered themselves to be responsible for the child with the drug problem and for the rest of the family. Being the brother or sister of a sibling with a drug problem did not carry these same responsibilities, which meant that they did not (and did not expect to) have an equivalent role in the decisions taken for the family by the parents. However, this did not mean that they passively accepted the family dynamic, or that their take on the situation was equivalent to that of their parents. This chapter will draw out the responses of brothers and sisters to the drug problems of their sibling in terms of how they felt it affected them, their family life and the relationships they had with their problem drug-using sibling.

As so many of the brothers and sisters interviewed had clear expectations of a 'normal' sibling relationship it is worth beginning by sketching this to illustrate their sense of contrast between their expectation and the perceived reality. The rest of the chapter will elaborate on the ways in which their sibling's drug problem got in the way of a positive relationship and was more broadly of social detriment to them.

A normal relationship

The great majority of brothers and sisters indicated that they had a strong sense of what they might expect of a sibling relationship were drugs not part of the picture. A normal sibling relationship was meant to be confiding, protective, interested and offering guidance and support. At core they held ideas that it was about a caring involvement with each other, which would outlast childhood fights and rivalries to mature into a confiding, trusting and friendly relationship. At one level, of course, these might just be a wish list of how things might be in a perfect world.

The wish of most siblings was for an elder brother and sister who was 'there' to listen to them, do things with them and broadly take an interest. The kind of mentoring role that elder siblings often take on with their younger brothers and sisters might be heard in the following description of a commonplace situation where the younger brother recalls the kinds of things he and his sister used to do before drugs took precedence in her life:

> *Em well when I wis like five and six she would take me out up tae Dennistoun wi' her pals and that, her friends and just hang about wi' them. I didnae really know then what was happening at that point. I was only young, I was only five or six or something like that. Ma sister used tae spike ma hair and stuff like that for me when I was younger.*
> (Sibling: Andrew)

The problem was that once drugs took centre stage then everything else, including them, was of secondary importance. Time spent together would fall away as their brother or sister became more and more absorbed by the business of getting money and buying and using drugs. This led to all the siblings characterising their drug-using brother or sister as selfish and having no sense of obligation to the family.

> *... I think when people, anybody, that starts takin' drugs, they totally lose all reality ... they do definitely change. Definitely, they become totally different people ... when they speak tae ye you dae feel as if they, they are the same person but a lot a things change ... wi' people that take drugs, it's as if they don't care for life at all, and they don't care about anybody else apart fae themselves basically.*
> (Sibling: Caroline)

There were a minority of siblings who had no expectations of the kind of 'normal' relationship they had lost or might achieve with their sibling. These siblings reported pre-existing animosity and distance from their brother or sister which stretched back into childhood.

> *I: ... Were you close to Tara as a child?*
>
> *R: I've never been close to Tara, never ... Mum says I've never liked her, even when I was in the pram I didnae like her.*
> (Sibling: Marie Louise)

It is perhaps noteworthy that reports of long-standing animosity towards brothers or sisters who had developed drug problems were most associated with those families that were reportedly the most dysfunctional, largely through parental drug or alcohol problems. The following extract, for example, describes aspects of the discordance of a family of eight brothers and sisters who grew up in a violent household where both parents had severe alcohol problems:

> *... We all started not really liking each other cause we've all got very different personalities ... You know, it's the most bizarre family I think ever, for personality wise. You know because everybody deals with the lack of emotional support from when we were younger in a different way. My big brother very rarely sees anybody, very rarely goes out the house. My big sister Sarah took a lot of drugs as well I think as an act, and my big sister Joan developed certain problems and we all just took on different personality traits you know.*
> (Sibling: David)

The drug problem (in this case of three siblings) certainly exacerbated these relational difficulties but these respondents were clear that drugs did not create them. Furthermore there was no evident notion that removing the drug problem would pave the way towards the creation of a positive bond between these siblings.

The deep familiarity that siblings have with each other through their shared experiences of growing up in the same family is part of what leads siblings into the expectation of being able to turn to each other to seek support and advice, and to share confidences. However, it was the distance between these expectations and their current relationships with brothers or sisters that was emphasised. One gets a clear sense of this from the reflections of the younger brother of a sister with a drug problem.

> *I: Do you ever sense that drugs have robbed you of a sister?*
>
> *R: I dae get that feeling. That feeling passed ma mind and I was just thinking tae maself 'What's these drugs done? This isnae ma sister that's staying wi' us'. It just wisnae*

like her wi' the problems and stuff. Just always naggin' ...

I: *And when you say that, what would you have wished her to be like with you?*

R: *Just wish she would be like ... just be like a normal sister, an older sister. I'd like to have been able to go tae her wi' problems but I cannae dae it for some reason, I don't know how ... I think it's because really that Andrea has got problems wi' the drugs and that and I don't want to hit her wi' other problems when she's got problems of her ain. I think it's that – I cannae be too sure.*
(Sibling: Andrew)

It was the loss of this caring involvement that was lamented by the brothers and sisters interviewed for this study. In the following extract a 13-year-old sister describes the difference in the relationship with her elder brother when he is using drugs to when he is not.

Like because me and Leanne [elder sister] *don't like really get along with him when ... he's using, but like when he's not, we do, we get along and ... we'll all like do stuff together like any other family but then when he's using we just don't seem to bother.*
(Sibling: Eleanor)

A recurrent complaint, particularly with the youngest siblings interviewed (13 years and up), centred on their perception of their brother or sister as fundamentally uninterested in them. They felt that when on drugs their siblings did not want to talk or listen to them or to spend time with them, which, as can be heard in the following interview extracts, was experienced as frustrating and disappointing:

'Cos when he was on drugs you couldnae really talk to him, he was like sitting like that [head down], *when you're talking to him you'd feel as if you were talking to yourself.*
(Sibling: Dean)

Because like ... he'll talk to you more when he's clean and ... I don't know, like you feel as if he's understanding you more better, – like you talk to him and he'll want to do things and that and then when he's no' he's just like cannae be bothered wi' ye.
(Sibling: Eleanor)

In addition to feeling that their drug-using sibling was uninterested in them, they felt that when on drugs they were very quarrelsome. One 13 year old described her brother as arguing over anything and everything when he was on drugs. Such discord was itself unwelcome but the siblings were especially aggrieved when the force of the argument was directed at parents and in particular their mothers.

He was just total ... evil and he thought he was always right and he never ever ... he just, once an argument started he would never back down from it. Like even when my mum had ... he would go to my mum 'shut up' and then it would get to the stage he would actually lose it, shout and bawl. If my mum went like that, 'right, just get oot the hoose' he would shout the whole way down the close, 'cos it was like a house like this, these closes are the exact same as up there, so it was like a house like that apart fae on that side, so the whole way doon the close and the whole way doon the street he'd be shouting 'ya fucking bitch' and ... know, name calling and whatever. So...
(Sibling: Martina)

The siblings (bar those few with no continuing relationship with their parents) were protective and defensive of their parents whom they considered were the most affected emotionally and otherwise.

> *I wis angry with* [Emma, sister] *no' so much ma da ... but wit she wis putting ma mum through.*
> (Sibling: William)

This might lead the non-drug-using sibling to come to the defence of the parent but often at the cost of further adding to the discordance:

> *I used to, like because he always used to upset my mum and I didnae like it ... Yeah, like I don't know, I feel it would upset my mum, I'd say something and then like try and tell him to like no' be so nasty but he never used to listen, then it used to be ma fault.*
> (Sibling: Eleanor)

Virtually all of the siblings referred to a tendency on the part of their brother or sister to feel sorry for themselves and furthermore blame everyone else for their problems past or present. This aspect of their brother's or sister's behaviour was described as highly irritating.

> *... She's always blaming it on you when it's always herself ... It really makes me mad 'cos she can't ... she always blames everybody else, 'it's your fault, you done this blah blah blah' but if she really didn't want to be on drugs she could stop, she could try and ... even though it's hard for her ...*
> (Sibling: Danielle)

As is apparent from the previous interview extract it is not that there was no appreciation of the difficulties siblings faced in living with a drug problem or indeed in trying to get off drugs. Frustration with these aspects of their drug-using sibling's behaviour was linked to the overall perception of brothers and sisters as having become completely preoccupied by drugs and self-absorbed in the process. This preoccupation to their minds led their drug-using siblings away from being concerned with, or for the family and in myriad ways corroded the fabric of their relationships with each other.

> *... Even up until today he's had ten million chances wi' us all and he's stole, he's done many things tae us all, he's said things, he's lied, he's always lookin' for a sympathetic vote. He gives ye all this an' all that but everybody's had a hard life so why should we all sit and give him any different?... I think he's wantin' attention or somethin', I think he feels that he's left out but he's no' left out, it's just the life he's livin' and naebody's interested. So we're supposed tae be pals wi' somebody we don't really like? Maybe if he changes his attitude a bit maybe we will start visiting him, maybe if he gets a grip of his life, get hisself a hoose, things like that, a wee job and maybe we'll go oot at the weekend and get a drink, things like that, I'll come up and visit him in his hoose if he can maybe get his life the 'gether* [together], *know wit I mean?*
> (Sibling: Stuart)

What this amounted to was a disinclination to spend anything other than a minimum of time with brothers or sisters when they were using drugs.

Worry and anxiety

Much the same as their mothers and fathers, these siblings worried about the health and well-being of their brothers and sisters when they were using drugs and away from home. When they disappeared for periods of time there would be anxiety that something had happened to them.

> *Of course, you're feart if they go out and doesn't come back the night, it's like where is he, where is he? Like now.*
> (Sibling: Martina)

> *Aye but you do worry about your brother because yer brother's yer blood ain't he? That's what I say, blood.*
> (Sibling: Liam)

Some siblings felt they had to a degree become accustomed to a pattern of absence and return which lessened their anxieties:

> *Aye I did worry about her to an extent because ye didnae know where ye were and naebody could get in contact wi' her and what no'. I suppose that was a wee bit worrying. But now it doesnae bother me because I know she'll be back and … God forbid somethin' did happen, but nothin' ever has.*
> (Sibling: Nick)

Most commonly the siblings in this study spoke of an anxiety that their brother or sister would overdose from drugs.

> *Like, it, it just eh like … ran through your head all the time* [worry about overdose] *and you used to like try and block it but … it'd just always be there.*
> (Sibling: Eleanor)

One brother appeared particularly anxious as to the well-being of his brother to the extent that he felt it interfered with his ability to concentrate at school and indeed interrupted many other aspects of his life:

> *R: It was affecting everything. I just didnae feel like daeing anything at all. Just couldnae stop thinking about it.*
>
> *I: And what couldn't you stop thinking about?*
>
> *R: The way … what's gonna happen to him, when is it ever gonna stop? Just things like that … 'Cos I know that drugs can kill you and if they kept going on and on it's just gonna affect them, you can kill yourself. I felt as if he was gonna kill hisself … but there was nothing I could dae 'cos he just wouldnae listen to me, every time I was mentioning it to him. He just wouldnae listen to me …*
> (Sibling: Dean)

The powerlessness of their position as siblings to alter things was also a theme in these interviews. Many siblings felt like helpless spectators in the unfolding drama of their brother's or sister's lives.

Living with public reactions to sibling drug use

There was universal reluctance among siblings to publicly acknowledge that a family member had a drug problem. This was entirely understandable given the likelihood of negative reactions from others, but was also related to the sense of shame felt by family members:

> *I: What was the kind of reason … I mean I know it's obvious but if you had said 'Why have you kept it quiet?'*
>
> *R: No wantin' anybody to know I suppose. Just trying tae keep the … Just tae let people know that the family was normal.*

That just like ... naebody did anything like that.
(Sibling: Nick)

Having a brother or sister with a drug problem was both shaming and embarrassing. It was embarrassing to see them in public under the influence of drugs or begging in the streets. This was true of all the siblings interviewed for this study:

But eh if I was tae see him in the street and he was mad wi' it I wid just ignore him. He'd be like that tae me 'awright Martin, how ye doin'' and I wid just ignore him. 'Martin! Martin! Martin! Martin!' ... And he'd be 'aye you fuckin' think yer better than me, who dae ye think ye are' and then afore ye know it the full street's fuckin' attracted tae him tryin' tae get a reaction oot a you and this is just because ye don't want tae talk tae him, because he's mad wi' it and he's gonnae ask ye for money or he's gonnae say 'I'm starvin', I've no' ate for two days' which is a total lie because he'll just go roon tae ma Ma's when ma Da's van isnae there and ma Ma'll feed him or give him fuckin' a big bag a messages [shopping] [laughs] *ye know.*
(Sibling: Martin)

The most likely reported response of siblings if they encountered their brother or sister in the street whilst under the influence of drugs would be to try to ignore them and slip out of sight so as to avoid any public humiliation.

I: And what's it like if you see him outside?

R: I find it embarrassing.

I: Embarrassing? And so then what would you do if you saw him?

R: I'd walk the opposite way.

I: You'd walk the opposite way. And would he see you?

R: Sometimes, and I'd just ignore him.
(Sibling: Eleanor)

As the following two siblings make clear, however, it is not just being under the influence of drugs that is the problem, but that the lifestyle associated with the drugs might mean that little attention has been paid to personal appearance and hygiene:

Naebody knows he's ma brother but if I wis tae walk about wi' him and he looked the way he's lookin', aye, he wid embarrass us 'cos ye just need tae look at him and you'd say 'aye', ye can tell by just lookin' at a person if they're a junkie or no'.
(Sibling: Stuart)

I'm so embarrassed [laughs]. *Barry had got a loan, a budget loan fae the Social tae get em ... an' he's said tae me 'I need new trainers an' can ye take me intae the Town Centre?' An' I says 'aye well come through' an' I went in an' I'm so embarrassed because he came in an' he'd no' shaved and ... dirty an' he's sayin' tae the man in the shop, em, 'have ye got any cheap caps, naw cheaper than that' and it's that voice an' I wis just so embarrassed, that's more the way I'm embarrassed wi' them.*
(Sibling: Caroline)

The unkempt appearance of a brother or sister was one thing; however, it was perhaps more socially destructive to have to run the gauntlet of those neighbours and others who considered they had been the victims of antisocial behaviour on the part of their sibling:

I get slagged noo and again, people say 'where's your brother that steals aff washing lines?' and all that, 'cos they know about it, a lot of people know about it, and I got all the stick for it 'cos they don't stay here, I need to live here, so it's me that gets all the stick for it.
(Sibling: Dean)

More serious consequences followed where they ended up embroiled in drug-linked violence because they happened to be related:

The guy hit him [his brother] *wi' it* [baseball bat] *o'er the heid, 'ya fuckin' bastard ye, Pollock', blah blah, I mean I wis about 14, 15, I wis like that ... and then the other guy jumped oot the other side and he's got this big knife an' he's runnin' at me, I don't know this guy, I've never done anythin' tae him but, an' is he gonnae use this on me just because I'm wi' him, just because I'm his brother? I don't deserve that, naebody deserves that. So Sean's like that tae me, 'run, fuckin' run, run', so I ran and the guy chased me maybe fuckin' twenty feet ... there wis absolutely nae way he wis catchin' me.*
(Sibling: Martin)

The above scenario was not commonly reported in this study. However, younger males were most likely to refer to their increased vulnerability to violence from other males as a result of the conflicts created by an elder sibling's drug-related and other behaviours.

The closeness just fell away 'cos he just caused trouble for us. Once he went [left the area] *we got bullied, first it was my brother Luke and then when he went into the army it was me. These boys used to wait for us when we came back from school and would give us a doin', it got to the point that you couldn't even go out to the shops 'cos they'd be waiting for you.*
(Sibling: Simon)

Partly their grievance seemed to reside in the notion that an elder, particularly male, sibling ought to be protective of the family interests. Their behaviours, far from protecting, could expose younger siblings to the violence of others.

What is lost and what can be recovered

But I was close to her when I was younger, I still am to this day. But there's days where I cannae stand tae look at her. But I think that's just 'cause I dae love her so much that I feel that way about her at times.
(Sibling: Nick)

The majority of brothers and sisters interviewed in this study attached great value to the sibling relationship and retained a strong sense of the person within, untainted by drugs. The damage done to the family and to their relationships with each other was not seen as irrevocable in most cases. However, positive change to their relationships with siblings was tied to a move away from problem drug use:

R: *... When she's in* [rehabilitation centre], *she phones a lot and she wants tae talk tae me and at Christmas when we went to her house for dinner she was talkin' tae me and that and sayin' that she wanted tae make up for lost time.*

I: *Yeah. What did you feel about that?*

> R: *I wis happy because I thought that she would get better and that me and her could be more like sisters and bond a little bit more.*
> (Sibling: Danielle)

The continued use of drugs was identified as causing the greatest damage to their sibling relationships and some saw the possibility that it could create a permanent wedge between them. Some siblings, however, felt their relationship had suffered too much damage as a consequence of the drugs and considered it to be irretrievably lost:

> *Me and Sam will never ever be close again, we talk you know, we're civil to each other now, but you can see it; there is no bond there. I would never ever want anything bad to happen to him you know, but at the same time I really wouldn't be surprised if something did ... There isn't very much love between me and Nick now and there's certainly no trust.*
> (Sibling: David)

Most siblings had not suffered so great a loss of faith in their brother or sister; most carried on with the belief that over time the brother or sister they remembered or wished for would return.

Conclusion

Siblings occupy difficult terrain: their brothers or sisters develop problems that absorb family time and energy, and place so many demands on the parents, particularly mothers. To an extent they become reluctant onlookers upon the developing family situation, as much of what happens is between the parent and the drug-using child. The stresses and strains described by so many parents in the preceding chapter affected the family dynamic and the quality of the home environment that siblings lived within. It is perhaps testimony to the rather anomalous position of siblings that so few had really considered how the drug problem of their brother or sister actually affected them. On the whole their concerns were directed outwards to how the mother was coping or not, or to concern for their drug-using sibling. Yet for all this it is clear that the drug and other problems of their siblings affected them greatly, whether in terms of getting in the way of things they wanted or needed to do (study for examinations, for instance) or because it diverted parental attention they felt they needed. Also it was clear that most siblings lamented the loss of a valued relationship with an elder sister or brother in whom they could confide and share positive experiences.

Of course, where siblings themselves developed drug problems, their lifestyles took on similar trajectories to those of their already drug-using siblings. It is to this issue that the next chapter turns attention.

4 The impact of exposure to sibling drug use

Introduction

The likelihood that other siblings in the same family will use drugs is the question that has received greatest attention from research on sibling drug use. By way of an answer, the almost exclusively quantitative research does indicate an increased likelihood of more than one sibling in a family having a drug problem. However, the processes by which more than one sibling in a family comes to have a drug problem are more opaque. Qualitative research has an important contribution to make in elucidating the processes by which family members' drug use may influence the drug-related attitudes and behaviour of other members of the family.

In the present study, 24 index sibling problem drug users were interviewed; of these ten reported having a brother or sister with a current or past problem with drugs. Clearly then this study is supportive of the general trend evident in the literature. For example, the DORIS (Drug Outcomes Research in Scotland) study, which is following the treatment careers of 1,000 problem drug users in Scotland over time, shows that of the 95.2 per cent of drug users who reported having siblings, just under a third (31.2 per cent) reported having at least one sibling who had ever had a problem with drugs and a further 8.6 per cent reported having ever had a problem with drugs and alcohol (personal communication: Neil McKeganey, 2004).

This chapter examines the narratives provided by the sibling with the drug problem (the index case) and the other sibling interviewed. These narratives are used to consider the nature of the influence that the person with the drug problem has had on younger brothers' and sisters' drug use, whether to encourage or prevent it. The literature on initiation of drug use by siblings has identified two factors as potentially influential: role modelling and advocacy. The influence of an older brother to model drugs positively and furthermore to actively encourage siblings to initiate drug use is predictably part of the dynamic that leads other siblings into using drugs. However, it is clear, from these data at least, that neither is determinate but highly contingent upon both the family environment and the quality of relationships between siblings and between siblings and their parents. The following section looks in some detail at varying levels of drug exposure and its consequences reported by the 24 index cases and the 20 other siblings with the aim of disentangling some of these processes.

Exposure to drugs

It is possible to discern two kinds of exposure to sibling drug use: routine, everyday kinds of exposure, and deliberate exposure where for different reasons the drug-using sibling takes the decision to directly involve the non-drug-using sibling in their drug-using lifestyle. Both kinds of exposure, however, could (and did) result in drug initiation of the other sibling. Almost all of the index siblings reported that their brother or sister had been exposed to their drug use to some degree. At minimum this involved seeing the effects of the drug use on their behaviour but more usually also involved having seen drugs and the paraphernalia associated with drug use, and often too having been present whilst they were being used. Five of the index siblings reported that none of their siblings had seen drugs or drug use, through either their own efforts at secrecy, their exclusion from the family home or the strict enforcement of rules restricting use of drugs whilst in the home.

Routine exposure to drug use refers to the kinds of everyday ways in which siblings sharing the same house or seeing each other fairly regularly might be exposed. The index siblings made frequent reference to the use of drugs whilst in the home and often whilst caring for younger siblings. Some spoke about trying to keep their drug use concealed from their younger brothers and sisters.

> *I:* *How much did they* [two young brothers] *actually see of your drug use?*
>
> *R:* *They didnae, they didnae … I wis babysitting the weans and … I would have ma stuff, right? What I've got and I'd have already taken it and then my ma would mibbae arrive in fae school 'Gonnae watch them for an hour?' Or she'd be goin' tae the Bingo about 6 o'clock 'Would you babysit them the night?' 'Aye nae bother.' And she would leave and I'd be 'alright' and then she'd be back and I'd be full o' it. But the weans would be out playing or wi' Archie or whatever. Or else I'd get them settled in front o' a video and then I'd dug* [locked] *ma door d'you know what I mean? They just never got to see it.*
> (Index sibling: Nadine)

In the above example the drug use was kept out of sight of the respondent's younger brothers. However, this seemed difficult to sustain:

> *I:* *Yeah but have you ever seen her using heroin or anything?*
>
> *R:* *Naw I've never seen it.*
>
> *I:* *Do you think she keeps it away from you?*
>
> *R:* *She does. But it wis a good few years ago before ma mum and dad really found out about it. I wis staying wi' ma sister and I wis just looking through her cupboard and I found a teaspoon aw burned at the bottom. That wis one thing that made me click on that she wis using somethin' … because that wis unusual. I've only ever seen that in like drug adverts or somethin' like burning heroin wi' a spoon and I wis like 'Yeah wait a minute'. But I kept it tae maself, I let it pass so I did.*
> (Sibling: Andrew)

Some index siblings described having used heroin in front of their younger siblings but had tried to pass off the drug as something else, usually as cannabis or cannabis oil:

> *But see ma wee brother at ten … I took him aw the time and watched him. I took him for two weeks here and weeks there and ma wee brother's … I used to … I've done it in front of him every day and he knows aw about it. I told him it wis hash at first and he's like that 'That's no hash, I know what that is. I've seen it on the polis stuff that they bring to school'.*
> (Index sibling: Vicky)

The success of such efforts at subterfuge was obviously dependent on the lack of knowledge of the other sibling, which was clearly not the case for this boy. There was also the ever-present possibility that a younger sibling might unsuspectingly be exposed to a sibling's use of drugs as in the case below:

> I: *And how much has Brenda been exposed to your drug use?*
>
> R: *She's only ever seen me once ever dain it and I had sent her in the kitchen tae make a cup o' tea and I wis like that 'She'll be standin' in there for a couple eh minutes.' And I had just woke up and I wis gonna dae ma hit and a had the tourney on and I had the pin in ma arm. She walked in and I fucking went radio rental. I just pulled out the pin in ma arm and I wis like 'Get the fuck back intae that kitchen.' She wis like 'I didnae see nothing.' I wis like 'I don't give a shit whether ye seen anything or no'. 'So she went back in the kitchen and I done ma hit and I went in and apologised for losing the rag wi' her. But I wis like that 'I don't want ye tae see me dain it. I might be a heroin addict but I don't want ye watching what I'm dain.'*
> (Index sibling: Evie)

Sometimes too the will to conceal the drug use was absent.

> I: *Right, right. So she knows what it* [the drugs] *was and all that?*
>
> R: *Aye she knows what it wis but again I didnae care because I wis needing it and I wis taking it. And I wisnae caring, I wouldnae have cared if it wis my ma that wis sitting there.*
> (Index sibling: Vicky)

One sister recounted the point from which she ceased to try to hide her drug use from her younger brother and openly used in front of him. As she herself points out, this came about through not sustaining the care to keep it hidden:

> *Now, whenever he walked in my room I'd be like* [gasps] *and I'd hide it or I'd drop it so he never seen it but ... I remember he walked into my room one day and I just didnae care. I just sat there like that and I went ... I stopped tooting and I looked and went 'what is it?' and he's like ... pure ... he didnae know what to say. He went 'oh, forget it' and he walked out.*
> (Index sibling: Mandy)

Where younger children were in the care of their older drug-using siblings they could be exposed to drug use outside the home too. For instance, this now 13-year-old girl revealed how, unbeknown to her mother, at an early age she and her nephew (son of her drug-using sister) were often taken to houses where drugs were being dealt and used:

> I: *What kind of things were you seeing?*
>
> R: *Like I saw Amanda taking drugs, heroin and stuff and I saw her boyfriend.*
>
> I: *How was she taking it?*
>
> R: *Injecting it in her arms and she was, em, burnin' it and smokin' it and stuff.*
>
> I: *Right. And was she trying to hide it from you?*
>
> R: *No, not ... sometimes, sometimes she did.*
>
> I: *And when was it you were seeing it and where were you?*

> R: *Oh ... she used tae go out and do it and she took me out one day and she was like going intae people's houses and she was leaving me in other rooms, know when I was older, she was leaving me in rooms but I can remember when I was younger she'd do it in like stairwells of people's closes* [tenement flats] *... And I wis like beside her.*
> (Sibling: Danielle)

These data also appear to indicate a greater routine exposure to drugs in families where one or both parents were preoccupied with their own drink or drug problems. Parental inattention and a lack of effective parental monitoring have been identified in a number of studies as strengthening the negative influence of others, including older siblings and peers (Duncan *et al.*, 1996; Vakalahi, 2001).

> R: *Well ... see when, eh, my mum was on the drink? She would let all o' us in and my wee sister would be there and there'd be a few users in the house, and aw the drunk people. And my mum knew it would be going on, like jagging* [injecting] *in the bedroom and ... she knew Colette was there but she ... she just ... kept drinking.*
>
> I: *Kept drinking?*
>
> R: *Aye, just didnae bother her. She wouldnae allow it when she was sober. D'you know what I mean?*
> (Index sibling: Annette)

These were also the households that, on the basis of the descriptions provided by the index siblings, were the most chaotic. It was through living in such a household that a drug-using sibling made the decision to allow her (then 9-year-old) sister to be present whilst she used drugs. Her reasoning led her to believe that transparency was preferable:

> *... So her Mum and Dad were jagging and they were puttin' her out the room all the time and then I started smokin' ma kit and I tried tae put her out the room one day, I says 'Ruth gonnae go in that room and sit the now hen, just five minutes' and she looked at me wi' a look on her face that I'll never forget as if 'no' you as well Sinead, no' ma big sister, you're no' daen the same as wit ma Mum and Dad are doin' are ye?' and I shouted her back in ... I says tae her 'Ruth, ye know wit I dae wi this don't ye?' And I pointed tae the foil, em, she says 'uh-huh' and I says 'well look I don't want tae put ye out the room, I don't want tae', I says so 'see it's up tae you, I'm givin' you the choice, ye can either go and sit in the living room for five minutes, just 'til I'm done or ye can sit there and watch the telly and don't bother, just sit and watch the telly in beside me and she went 'can I just sit here and watch telly?' I said 'of course ye can'.*
> (Index sibling: Sinead)

Where younger brothers and sisters are routinely exposed to drugs there is the chance that they will develop a curiosity as to their effects and that this might encourage experimentation. There is also the possibility that a sibling's use of drugs such as heroin might conceivably normalise its use such that taboo warnings against heroin use would be rendered ineffective. The interviews with younger siblings indicated in particular the degree to which proximity to drugs played a role in encouraging a curiosity that resulted in experimentation and the development of drug dependence. In the case of Annette's young sister Colette, cited above, and also Barry watching his older brother with his friends, there was an interest in what was going on:

> *And he used tae just sit in an' he wid be puffin cannabis and maybe takin' the odd bit of speed and ... well I used tae go in an' chap the door, curiosity ... I'd want tae sit in wi' them but I wis never allowed tae ... the odd time, the odd time he wid say 'aye well ye can sit in for five minutes', 'cos I wis annoyin' them that much an' then pap us out again.*
> (Index sibling: Barry)

When Barry first bought and used heroin it was in the company of friends. However, he knew what to do and how to use it from having watched his brother use it for years before him. It was also through watching her brother smoke heroin and being curious as to its effects that Chantelle first used it:

> I: *And how much did you know what was going on?*
>
> R: *Em, quite a lot, he wid sit and dae it in front of me all the time, I used tae sit and say, 'gee's a smoke, gee's a smoke' and one time he did ... an' I wis sick!*
> (Index sibling: Chantelle)

Many siblings in this study, whether drug using or not, spoke of their expectations of an elder sibling as someone to look up to and be an example to them. When these elder siblings went on to use drugs problematically there were those younger siblings who modelled these behaviours. Chantelle explicitly acknowledged this, as did other interviewed siblings. It would not necessarily be the older sibling who actually initiated the drug use: this could happen with peers. However, being consistently exposed to drugs and drug taking might work at an insidious level to demystify drug use, to teach its use and through proximity make possible their casual experimentation without fully understanding the possible personal consequences of such action. Other research (Brook *et al.*, 1983; Needle *et al.*, 1986) has indicated that the likelihood of multiple sibling drug use is greatly increased when the younger brother or sister is also associating with deviant peers, which underlines the important interconnections between sibling and peer influences.

Deliberate exposure

This section considers those accounts in which drugs (or their effects) were deliberately shown to siblings and in four cases their use was deliberately advocated. The motives for deliberate exposure were not solely about encouraging use. Indeed in a number of cases it was intended to have the opposite effect on the likelihood that a sibling would experiment with drugs such as heroin.

Perhaps the starkest example of a sibling advocating drug use can be found in the following interview excerpt. The index sister related how she was responsible for inducting two of her nine siblings into heroin use on the basis that it was an improvement on the substances they were already using:

> R: *I kind o' got my brothers into smack, but anything else they got theirselves into. I think it was me that get them intae the smack ...*

I: *OK, so there's three of you. How did you get them into it?*

R: *Well I didnae get them intae it, just kind o' introduced them tae it. If they were coming doon to my hoose I was gieing them a ... charge, it just ended up wi' a habit ...*

I: *So which one was it that got into it first?*

R: *Em, my older brother. I got him into it first.*

I: *How did that happen, do you remember?*

R: *He was on the glue and I used to say to him 'fling the glue bag away and I'll gie you a shot o' this'. Just used to, like get him to fling his glue bag away and I'd gie him a charge and then he just ended up in about it.*

(Index sibling: Lynette)

It needs to be added that, by her account, Lynette's family had a number of serious problems, particularly the severe alcohol dependence on the part of the mother and the numerous partners who had separately fathered each of the nine children. The other reported cases where siblings were introduced to drugs by their siblings were less overtly bleak, couched within frameworks of self-interest or even, as will be described, the sibling's protection.

In the following case Richard described how his elder brother introduced him to drugs, reportedly to compromise him. Admiration of his elder sibling was part of Richard's explanation for his initiation into heroin: 'If my big brother done it I would dae it'. However, he also considered that his elder brother's self-interest was part of the explanation for his initiation into heroin use; as is clear from the following narrative account. When Richard threatened to tell his mother that he had found his elder brother using drugs, his brother responded by tricking him into using heroin, which therefore implicated Richard in the act.

I used to blackmail him stupid. I used to always go 'if you don't dae this for me I'm telling my ma' and he used to dae it for me. So I was like 'I'm gonna tell her that'. And he jumped and he's like that, 'gonnae no' tell her, gonnae no' tell her', he's like that, 'look, try it it's hash oils'. He gave me two lines and I started being sick all over the place. 'How do I get this away?' and he's like that, 'you need to take mair' and he was gieing me mair and I'm whiteying [passing out] *all over the place, so ... this was eh ... just before I was 16 and I hated it. I says 'I'm no taking it any mair, I don't want any' and he went 'you tell my ma that I took it, I'll tell my ma that you took it'.*

(Index sibling: Richard)

A non-drug-using sibling described a situation where her sister had offered her heroin, which to her mind was motivated by the desire to create parity between them where usually there was hostility and rivalry for the mother's attention:

A couple of times she offered me it ... Tara would have loved for me to have turned round and says aye because the whole ... she would've went right back and told my mum and dad like that, she'd have loved it just to have one up on me ...Sort of to say to my mum and dad 'well no she's not any better than me', but she never got that chance.

(Sibling: Marie Louise)

Self-interest was also what motivated one drug-using sibling directly to expose his sister to drugs because he could not go safely to the particular area where the drug dealer lived and he used her to buy them for him. Unbeknown to him she started to sample his heroin and developed a drug problem herself.

> *I ended up blaming maself for her tae start using because ... I couldnae go to a certain bit and I used to get her boyfriend to go and score for me and she'd go wi' him and bring it back to me so I think I might have introduced it d'you know what I mean? Getting her to go and score for me ... Then one time I walked in and I caught her wi' tin foil ... Then I knew. But I wisnie really bothered and aw that because I couldnae criticise her if I'm using. I wis injecting it and she wis only smoking it.*
> (Index sibling: William)

Perhaps the most unexpected rationale for deliberate exposure of drugs to siblings was that it would be preventive. In the following account a drug-using sibling describes how she tried to encourage her brother to take heroin with her so as to pre-empt any use elsewhere. In retrospect she herself found her reasoning to be bizarre and put it down to the fact that she was greatly under the influence of drugs herself at the time:

> *... I turned round to Nick and I went 'listen, you know what that is don't you?' and he went 'aye, it's smack' like that and I went ... I went 'aye, heroin, smack, whatever you want to call it'. I went 'Nick son, promise me you will never, ever go on that' ... But I said to him 'but Nick, what if one o' your pals ever offer you it? Curiosity does kill the cat, you know?' and I was like ... 'So like would you say no to your pal?' and he went 'none o' my pals touch it' ... And I says 'look' and I says – and I cannae believe I actually done this. I says 'look, do you want to try it the now so that you've tried it and then you can say "well at least I've tried it and I don't want to go near it"?' and he went 'no' and I went 'are you sure now 'cos you can just have ... I'll show you what to dae ... go, just have a wee shot and I'll ... then that way, you've tried it', and I'm saying 'I'll dae it for you and then that way you've tried it and you'll see what it's like and you won't, and then you'll no' need to try it again'. He went 'Mandy I'm no' fucking interested, leave me alone or you're no' getting this* [hash] *joint basically', and I went 'right, OK, fair enough, I've asked you'. And see when I think about it, thank God he never tried it because it's good and he'd have thought 'oh brilliant!' and he'd have kidded on to me, 'that's rubbish, I don't like that' but really inside he'd have been like 'wow, this is amazing!' and he might have ran out the next day to get some. So thank God.*
> (Index sibling: Mandy)

By any account this is an unusual means of trying to prevent drug use. However, many of the siblings with drug problems reported drawing deliberately on their experiences of drug dependency to try to discourage their brothers and sisters from using drugs themselves. This ranged from showing drug-related injuries to describing the effects of drugs:

> *But I've showed her my hole in my groin and I've said 'do you want to end up like that?' I can honestly say that I've got my wee brother and sister terrified of smack. The only way they would take smack is because I've been that open wi' them, I've writ them letters as in I've treated them like adults.*
> (Index sibling: Richard)

It is interesting to note that Richard's account shows both an awareness of the preventive role of exposure and its flip side, that in being open about his drug use he might also have created an attraction to them.

The siblings' reactions to these prevention activities were rather mixed. Many resented their problem drug-using sibling taking on the role of teacher given that these were lessons they themselves seemed unable to heed:

> *R:* *I just can't get my mind round how he wants to dae it ... But then like he would say to me 'never do it' and then like I'd say 'why do you do it?' and he just doesnae answer ye.*
>
> *I:* *Yeah. And does that annoy you?*
>
> *R:* *Aye, like he would tell me, he'd tell me off, but he does it.*
> (Sibling: Eleanor)

Indeed the following sister makes clear that such advice was entirely counterbalanced by the lessons she drew from her brother's behaviour rather than his words to the contrary:

> *... 'Cos like my brother never, ever gave me it or anything or like the guy that I was seeing never, ever gave me it. They just says like 'don't take it' but at the end of the day they were sitting taking it in front of me so ... I was like, well, if they can take it how can I no' take it? Know what I mean, it can't be that bad. It's like if somebody smokes and they're sitting smoking a fag and they go 'don't smoke' ... 'uh uh'. 'It's bad for you, just learn fae my mistake' and you're like, 'mm, right, well ...' I just, I think that's rubbish, somebody saying that to you. I mean like 'don't smoke' and they're sitting wi a fag, I would go like ... swear at their wean and then you swear and they go 'don't swear' or something, know what I mean? It's ... contradicting yourself really innit? But that's what they were daeing so I tried it myself.*
> (Sibling: Martina)

Situations where siblings are deliberately offered drugs by brothers or sisters, often in the context of the home environment, have to be seen as posing a high risk of encouraging drug initiation as drugs are made freely available by trusted familiars. That such exposure would occasion the refusal of drugs is as important as those circumstances within which they are accepted. The following and final section considers the rationales for non-use of drugs that were offered by siblings.

Turning away from drugs

Analyses of the data on siblings both with and without a drug problem emphasised the difficulties in assuming that just because one sibling has a drug problem so another of their siblings will develop one. This research has indicated that siblings with brothers or sisters with drug problems are at elevated likelihood of developing drug problems themselves. Yet what of those other brothers or sisters who similarly had siblings with drug problems but who had not (at least at the time of interview) become drug involved? Consideration of the kinds of routine and deliberate exposure that these non-drug-using siblings experienced has indicated the increased pressures they face, some with less success than others. These pressures need to be accounted for in terms of both those siblings who succumbed and those that did not.

The biggest lessons that the siblings who did not take drugs learned were not as a result of any didactic role their drug-using sibling adopted. Instead they were influenced by the example and experience of their problem drug-using sibling. They looked at the appearance and behaviours of their siblings and took these as good reasons for not becoming involved in drugs:

> *... All you need to do is to look at the boy for an example and just see how he's fucked his own life up through drugs and how he's fucked his body up and how he's ... he wis a big boy know ... now he's just a wee skinny, scraggy wee junkie. Sells the Big Issue and that, know what I mean.*
> (Sibling: Stuart)

It was also their sense of the devastating impact that the drug use had on the family, particularly on their mothers, that affirmed their intention never to become involved in drugs:

> *I:* *That's the worst thing about it [drug use] for you?*
>
> *R:* *Ruin your life ... and you lose all your family. I seen what it done to Richard, he lost a lot of his family when he was on drugs. Naebody wants to know you. Steal and ... everywhere you go, everybody knows you. Just get booed and all that, battered and all that.*
> (Sibling: Dean)

There were those siblings who did not think they would ever have become involved in drugs because it was not in their natures. Their exposure to drug use would not to their minds alter that situation, although experiencing the impact that it had on the family might have hardened that resolve as in the case of Martin below:

> *... I've never ... I can honestly put ma hand on ma heart and say I've never tried any sort a drug, I've never tried smokin' a cigarette but just very seldom I wid take a drink ... I widnae say that wis because a ma brothers, it wis just ... it's somethin', it's just somethin' that's never really interested me ...*
> (Sibling: Martin)

Many siblings said they could not understand the attraction of drugs or the associated lifestyle. They saw their brothers or sisters as sad, angry people and considered that it was their drug problems that had largely brought this about. The fact that they could sacrifice so much for drugs was further underlined by witnessing them whilst 'full of it'; a state which from their perspective was neither fun nor sociable, as these two siblings explained:

> *I:* *What, what is your feeling about drugs?*
>
> *R:* *That I just wouldnae take them and ... I don't understand how like people want to go and dae it when you can like get more out o' life than sitting about taking drugs.*
> (Sibling: Eleanor)

> *... I don't know, I just ... I don't get the sense in sitting wi' your eyes shut and ... I'd rather be sitting gabbing away and ...* [laughs]. *Do you know what I mean?*
> (Sibling: Andrea)

These siblings provided compelling narratives of how exposure to the effects of drugs was a deterrent to experimentation. Yet there was no guarantee that this opposition to drugs would endure. For example, some of those siblings who had developed problems with drugs pointed to an earlier time when they had been similarly anti-drugs, often for reasons of close familial experience with their negative effects. There were those respondents who were so anti-drugs in their early years that they had been identified as the ASC (Anti Smack Crew):

> *... Chase them out my scheme* [housing estate]. *When I caught them I would ... leave them for deid, that's the truth. I would jump over their heids, trample them, my ma didnae know about any o' this, go through all their pockets and take all their tablets aff them, I would take their smack aff them, their heroin, and I'd put it doon a stank* [drain]. *And say 'oh ya junkie bastard' and aw that, 'get out our scheme' and all that. Having needles or anything like that, if I caught anybody jagging up a close* [shared stairwell of tenement flats] *in my scheme, I hated it. I hated junkies. I still hate it to this day. I might be a ... as in a junkie but I don't class myself as a junkie. I class a junkie somebody that lets theirself fall away.*
> (Index sibling: Richard)

There were also some index siblings who had experienced at first hand the negative impacts of drugs on their families, including the deaths of close family members, and yet they had gone on to develop drug problems despite this:

> *You would think I would have learned 'cos ... my auntie, my dad's sister ... died o' an overdose. My ma's sister has just came aff kit herself. Em ... my ma and ma da were both on it, so ... you would think that would teach you to say 'naw', you know what I mean but ... dunno.*
> (Index sibling: Shanice)

On the basis of these accounts one might feel less than sanguine about the curative powers of experiencing the negative effects of problem drug use, even at first hand, to prevent drug involvement.

Conclusion

The reasons why one sibling develops a drug problem but another does not appear to evade determination. Exposure to drugs and drug use through close proximity does seem to elevate the risk of drug initiation. Having an elder brother or sister using drugs in the home might excite the curiosity of a younger sibling and being in a familial relationship might legitimate experimentation and downplay the potential dangers. The degree of parental supervision and monitoring of the family situation, as well as the quality of the relationship between the parent figure and the sibling(s), might be factors contributing to the likelihood of sibling drug use whether directly through older siblings or more indirectly through their associations with friends engaged in problematic behaviours. The fact that many siblings resisted such pressures and did not become drug involved is important and probably connected to such dynamics as stability in the home environment over time, a commitment to conventional social values and friends who are not involved with deviant peer networks. For the rest, much may depend on the personality and drive of the brother or sister to negotiate a safe path away from drugs.

5 Practitioners' views on the family affected by problem drug use

Introduction

Although the report's main focus has been on the impact of a family member's drug problem on the family, consideration is also given to the perspectives of a small number of service providers and practitioners on the impact of drug problems on families. The tension between viewing the family as a potential resource in supporting the problem drug user and the negative impacts on the family as a result of offering such support was apparent in these interviews, as was the view that siblings were often largely tangential. Overwhelmingly there was a perception that the complexity of family dynamics and relationships invited great caution in involving other members of the family.

The views of the teachers, general practitioners (GPs), family support group members, social workers and drug workers reported here[1] have to be seen as offering no more than a small window into the response of practitioners. With the limitations of a small sample in mind, some observations are offered here. Predictably the professional remit of the service was instrumental in defining the nature and extent of the encounters with families with a problem drug-using member. Teachers were primarily concerned with the child to be educated; the prime concern of the drug workers interviewed was the person with the drug problem and, in this particular service, their dependent children. So too social workers were likely to have a focus on the child and provision of a safe supportive environment for the child in the shape of parents or grandparents. GPs, in offering generic services in the community, were likely to have a broader perspective on the issues for families from the perspectives of the person with the drug problem, their parents and any dependent children. The needs of the person with the drug problem, the enormous strains that their drug dependency problems imposed on their parents and the implications for child welfare were, with varying emphasis, key concerns across these professional and voluntary (family support) agencies. Siblings were not, however, prominent in their concerns. Where they were considered at all it was most likely to be in terms of the supportive role they could play.

The family as a resource and its limits

A common theme running through the interviews with general practitioners, drug workers and social workers was the perception of the family as a potential resource for the problem drug user. It was particularly the case that professionals would gravitate to concerns over the vulnerability of the problem drug user's children and emphasise the important support that a family could provide in protecting that child were the parent's drug problem to escalate.

> *We would try to encourage all these relationships because we think that the mothers would need as much help as they can get when they are outside* [leave the rehabilitation unit], *especially from family, because family will take the children and the children feel safe.*
> (Drug worker)

As brothers and sisters (and therefore as aunts and uncles of their sibling's children), there was the possibility that siblings could be a source of support in either helping overcome the drug problem or stepping in when their nieces and nephews needed help. However, closely allied to this was reflection on the strains this imposed on families and the possibility that such support could prove counterproductive.

> *These relationships often end up founded on disappointment where they've tried to support an individual, a brother or sister, where they've taken advice from an agency. Do they provide financial support? Do they provide a home for them? All sorts of things and then at various points along the way dependent on an individual's drug or alcohol use, the other sib may be disappointed by what happens.*
> (Social worker)

The finesse of the balancing act required by practitioners who were prepared to bring in the wider family was acknowledged in particular by a GP who, in working for over 20 years in the one community, had known many families over two to three generations. As he explicitly acknowledged, it was this depth of knowledge that gave him the confidence to judge when it might be feasible to suggest the potential strengths of other family members to help. This long experience of working with families where a son or daughter had developed a drug problem had led this GP to try to counsel parents and sometimes siblings too into taking account of their own needs, which included an appraisal of the balance between meeting the needs of the child with the drug problem and the destructive force of the drug problem on the family.

> *Then of course there's the appropriate response to it* [drug problem]. *How much do they seek to support, protect and how much do they seek to challenge and say this is not acceptable? Obviously it has put a lot of people through the absolute wringer over that one. At what point do they break? 'No, this is not acceptable, get out of my house', particularly when it's a mother telling that to a son or daughter. Obviously that happens frequently and obviously my role has been to tell people 'look at what you are feeling, trust your own instincts and if you feel this is leading to death and destruction for the whole family then you have to say it's the parting of the ways' ... That's the challenging part from my point of view, to judge that correctly.*
> (GP)

Where professional agencies might be inclined to see the family as a possible resource for the problem drug user, self-help family support groups in the voluntary sector were more inclined to emphasise the limits to that help and focus on the needs of the family left floundering in the wake of a child's drug problem. The notion of 'tough love' has often been articulated and espoused by members of the family support groups. As is self-evident from the name, the principal role carved out by the family support groups was as a resource for families, a place of respite peopled by those who had either lost their children to drugs through overdose or had lived with their drug problems, usually through many long years. Their often bitter experiences in trying to both help their children and retain some semblance of family life led to the conclusion that for many family members, if not most, it was an impossible balance.

We ask them [parents], *'What's changed? See all the stuff you've been doing? Has it changed them?' I say 'well what have you got to do? You need to change, you need to change the way you deal with them and the way you deal with the rest of the family. The stuff you've been doing, it's no' working' … We've got a saying here 'saying no helps, saying yes hurts'. The more you say yes to the addict the more life will hurt you.*
(Family support worker)

It was apparent from these interviews, and through observation, that the main users of this service were mothers; fathers were much less evident. The longevity of many of their children's drug problems also suggested that people either did not find their way to the family support groups in the beginning or were not able in the early phases of living with the drug problem to shift their focus from trying to help the child with the drug problem to helping themselves and their families.

Help for siblings

Aside from viewing the sibling as providing a source of support for their drug-using brother or sister there was not a great deal of practical consideration of the impacts of the drug problem on them. In part this might be explained by the lack of service contact with siblings: for example, in a rehabilitation unit for mothers and children other family members were described as 'shadowy people' and few service providers could recall having been approached directly by siblings regarding their brother's or sister's drug problem. One GP commented, 'Siblings are not a priority'. Undoubtedly this sentiment is based on an assessment of the vulnerabilities of dependent children and the compounding mental and physical health needs of parents presenting with stress-related problems such as angina and depression. However, as the other GP intimated, there was also stress and strain among siblings. This GP's recognition of how problem drug use could affect siblings meant that he tried to provide them with space for the expression of their often strong emotions; although, as is alluded to in the following extract, the duty of confidentiality to patients placed clear constraints on the scope for such intervention.

I mean I don't usually go out and beat the bushes to find the siblings. Usually the siblings find their way to me. So I really have to accept their agenda as to what they want to talk about. And very often they don't want to talk about the drug use in the family. So sometimes I have to bring up the subject, as it were, and just say something very loosely and just see what kind of reaction it creates. And if one immediately picks up that one is touching a very tender point then one has to go very gingerly. But it may be the most revealing bit of all, going into that. I mean generally speaking I allow them to express anger because quite often they've not been allowed to express anger or whatever. So, open up. I suppose I normally rehearse that kind of thing with them, as I do with death and what have you, the feelings of guilt and the feelings of anger etc. that are necessarily part of the reaction to a very disturbing situation.
(GP)

However, beyond this, the GP found it difficult to suggest any other supportive infrastructure within which siblings might find specific help. The two family support groups, although more than willing to involve siblings, usually in the form of a group, both recognised their limitations in this regard. One family support group had initiated a group for siblings, for example, but reported it had failed because of non-attendance. Their personal experiences led them to believe that most siblings responded by cutting off from their drug-using siblings. Although a number of practitioners made reference to support groups for siblings and other family members affected by alcohol problems (under the umbrella of Alcoholics Anonymous) they knew of no equivalent for drug-affected families. A family support worker felt that given the limitations of their ability to involve siblings directly they could help by encouraging parents to divert their intense focus on the drug-using child to the rest of the family:

> *I think that the best help for families is for parents to get a bit of help ... Get them to think about their other kids. What's their hobbies? What kinds of things do they like to do? And they don't know. See I done that with my own boys. I didn't know what they did.*
> (Family support worker)

The drug and social workers were aware of some of the pressures faced by siblings but were similarly at a loss as to how to involve them in their current remit. Where the drug worker spoke of the potential therapeutic value of introducing family group conferencing, for example, it was inevitably focused on the client group.

The perspective of the teachers was rather differently slanted, which reflected their professional commitment to educate all the children in their charge whatever their home circumstances. One headteacher whose school was in an area of high deprivation (which included high levels of problem drug use) spoke of the extra understanding staff would show to children whom they knew experienced family difficulties. On the whole they saw school as offering children a haven away from these difficulties.

> *I think that quite often they want to forget about it, they want to find out about the Romans, they want to go to PE and sometimes they don't want to think about all the hassle they have at home, because it's like six hours of escape in here and they get the opportunity to be children.*
> (Headteacher)

There was also an awareness of the limitations of their role, first in identifying problems where children were guarded about family difficulties and second in intervening with families (outside mandatory child protection responsibilities). As this headteacher remarked:

> *The school can support, help. You could probably have a bigger role in supporting children, or maybe supporting families to access other networks or places they could get help. But I do actually think a lot of the time the first step has to come from the families or the relatives. The other thing is if kids tell you something, not particularly scary like 'my big brother's doing that, doing that', but maybe not illegal, but generally I don't think you can get involved in everybody's life, try to sort out everybody's problems.*
> (Headteacher)

The headteachers saw educating the child in a safe learning environment as their primary task. One of the great strengths of the school environment was its inclusivity so that all children irrespective of their problems at home could benefit. Such a perspective ran counter to an especial singling out of groups, such as siblings with problem drug-using brothers or sisters.

Complex family dynamics

Awareness of the complexities of family dynamics was frequently referred to in these practitioner interviews. It prompted caution on the part of agencies in intervening with families in terms of either enlisting the help of siblings with their drug-using brother or sister or looking beneath the surface of narrated family histories. It is worth reiterating that since the direct remit of most of the practitioners was the individual's drug problem, their sense of the sibling was framed largely in terms of the help they might, or might not, provide to the drug user. The following interview extract shows this understandable focus but also indicates an appreciation of the factors limiting the sibling's ability to provide support:

> *... Because the help they* [family member] *can offer will always be complicated by the kinds of emotions of it, which is different from agencies where the emotional support is there but you are not emotionally tied to them as a person ... that takes its toll on the family member.*
> (Social worker)

Sentiments of anger and resentment, disappointment and sadness were attributed to the siblings in responding to their problem drug-using brother or sister and were seen as inevitably limiting the capacities of the siblings to provide support. Among those practitioners who had worked most closely and for many years with drug-affected families there was a depth of understanding of pre-existing tensions between siblings and how these greatly complicated the picture. As, for example, the following GP highlighted:

> *There's the usual thing between brothers and sisters etc. of the rivalries and the histories of things that have gone before. There's so many dynamics, from siblings who have always been very dominant so that the drug user has always been dominated by this and therefore is this the right thing to try and resuscitate? That dominant bit can go to full abuse. I mean we've got families where the elder sibs have abused physically and sexually or both, their own siblings as children. So, one has to be pretty careful about siblings, because it may not be the best thing to resuscitate something that is better left as history.*
> (GP)

Perhaps predictably it was the family support group members who most keenly appreciated the push and pull of sibling relationships, from their vantage point as parents. They understood that the drug problem compromised the relationships that brothers and sisters could have with each other and caused long-lasting damage that got in the way of their ability to provide the kinds of support that might ideally be given:

> *Siblings lose their relationships, their trust, they're always very wary of them. They lose their relationships where once they were close and now they're not. It's like a death, it really is. It's the end of relationships; they become different to them in a way that makes them very isolated. Devastating really.*
> (Family support worker)

Pre-existing tensions between siblings whether for attention or based on other rivalries once overlaid by the destructive forces of problem drug use made for a heady cocktail that cautioned practitioners in their dealings with families.

Conclusion

Practitioners are inevitably preoccupied with the needs of their client groups, most usually the problem drug user and parents (in practice, mothers) in the case of GPs and the family support workers. The needs of siblings affected by their brother's or sister's drug problem rarely seem part of the equation. Where they are considered it is most likely to be in terms of the support they might provide in helping their brother or sister to recovery. The next and final chapter brings the report to a close by considering what kinds of support might be made available to siblings as well as concluding more broadly what families might need both in coping with family members who develop drug problems and in preventing drug initiation by other siblings.

6 Conclusion

This study has offered a glimpse of the impact that problem drug use has on families. The two main areas of focus throughout have been, first, the impact of the drug problem on the family, and more specifically siblings, and second, a consideration of the likely influence of proximity and exposure to drugs through having a sibling involved in problem drug use. This concluding chapter will briefly summarise the main findings in each of these areas and consider what these data might indicate by way of possible responses from the point of view of policy and intervention. At this point it is salutary to keep in mind the enormity of what it is that parents and siblings have to confront when a son or daughter, brother or sister develops a drug problem. Grafting a solution onto something as complex as the way in which a family responds to problem drug use, whilst perhaps an instinctual reaction, requires acceptance of the paucity of our understanding. There is still far too much that we do not know to be confident of intervention with these families. The ways in which services might mesh with families, and the reach and efficacy of these services, are largely unknown quantities.

How do drugs affect families and what is the scope for help?

Problem drug use is clearly experienced as highly stressful by all close family members. Its intractability and the seemingly relentless chain of negative events set in motion by the development of a drug problem by a son or daughter, brother or sister appear to have severe and enduring impacts on family functioning as well as on the social lives and on the physical and mental health of those family members who struggle to come to terms with and adapt to the effects of the drug problem on all their lives.

Chapters 2 and 3 outlined the volatile mix of anger, sadness, anxiety, shame and loss that parents and siblings reported in their experience of having a close family member with a drug problem. Families reported disarray upon discovering the extent of the drug problem, usually because of a lack of knowledge of problem drug use and its seriousness and out of a sense of being overwhelmed by what they were witnessing in their relative. At most, parents would consult with GPs for help and advice with their child's drug problem but more usually the family response was to turn in on itself and try to solve the problem with its own resources. The often felt shame of having a child with a drug problem further cemented the impulse to keep the problem within the family. It was not usual for parents at this stage to access sources of support outside the family, perhaps because their focus was the child with the drug problem, not the effects on themselves and the family.

The continued use of drugs by the family member, despite help or opposition, left families feeling an acute impotence to alter the course of the drug problem. Parents lamented the loss of the child that was and most siblings reported sadness at the loss of a valued relationship. Witnessing their child or sibling becoming more enmeshed by their drug problem, they had a sharp sense of the vulnerability this created through involvement in criminality, homelessness, hospitalisation, violence and the risk of death through overdose or contraction of disease, but felt powerless to alter its course.

Families universally reported conflict and strain in their relations both with the drug-affected member and with the rest of the family. Arguments seemed to rage between parents and the problem drug-using child over their continued drug use or stealing or problems with police and so on. Parents reported bitter and often destructive disagreement over how best to respond to the child with the drug problem and siblings would argue with the problem drug-using brother or sister and with their parents over their treatment of the drug-using sibling. The push and pull over whether to help, to what extent and in what ways was an ongoing dialectic creating a good deal of stress between family members. Furthermore the tendency of the family member's drug problem to take centre stage drained parental time and energy, resulting in an imbalance in the attention and other resources available for other siblings. The family support worker's comment 'it's the end of relationships' encapsulates the sense of family dissolution reported by most of the parents and siblings who were interviewed.

Family support groups

The easiest recommendation would be for some more formal recognition and a funding role for the many locally run self-help family support groups in assisting these families. It is certainly true that many, if not most, of the parents who regularly meet at the family support groups find them to be useful and often highly supportive. However, without much information on the ways in which groups are run, who they work with and to what ends, this recommendation needs some firmer evidence base from which to work. As self-help groups they are often self-funding and this, combined with often informal leadership, means that they may be quite short-lived. For example, in ringing around a current list of satellite family support groups in the Glasgow area it became quickly apparent that many had ceased to exist because of both funding problems and the changed priorities of the main stakeholder. This latter suggests a certain inevitable fluidity in the membership and make-up of local community-run family support groups in particular, which affects their administration and longevity. Further, family support groups seem mostly made up of mothers and frequently they have lived with their child's drug problem over many years. Fathers are much less in evidence and I have never seen any evidence that the brothers or sisters of drug users had any specific input.

- These factors suggest that a first step in looking to recognise more formally the role of the family support groups might be to assess the remit and capacities of a range of such groups in different geographical localities in terms of their funding, their membership, their longevity and, most importantly, what past and present members consider to be of value, or not, to them and their families.

Respite

The many strains of living with a family member's drug problem create an environment that is stressful for parents and children. Furthermore the drug problem with all its attendant crises effectively distracts attention from other family relationships. Providing the family with the opportunity to have some time away from their situation and take some leisure was greatly appreciated by families but all too rarely enjoyed. One of the mothers I contacted, for example, had managed to scrape together enough money to take her daughter and resident grandson on a three-night coach tour to London. It was almost beyond her means but she had done this to lighten the loads of the children and, by taking them out of their situation, she had given them the opportunity to focus on each other and just have fun. Although a modest suggestion in that it does not set anything permanently in place, it offers families the opportunity to find some breathing space for themselves.

- Respite for families offers a low-key but probably highly valued intervention for families to escape the sometimes intolerable stresses brought about by a close family member's drug use.

Reaching siblings

Siblings clearly are negatively affected by the experience of having a brother or sister with a drug problem, both because it impacts on the family and its functioning and because of the loss of a valued relationship. However, it is difficult to see how one could engage siblings in services devised specifically for them. In a sense to do so contributes to the problem, already identified in this research, of atomising the individual. Siblings tend not to construe the problem as being about them but about their drug-using brother or sister. Their view very largely seemed to be that if the drug problem were to be resolved so would the family problem. To engage the sibling in services would require that they be construed as a problem but this research, at least, indicates that, although obviously the family dynamic affects them, they are more onlookers than directly involved. This does of course bring its own issues to bear but it is difficult to see how services could really intervene to resolve this, except perhaps by the use of mentors.

Also on what basis would such siblings be identified? The stigma of problem drug use makes it unlikely that they would volunteer publicly their sibling's drug problem and any other method would require the involved professional (for example a teacher) to know the family history.

- The opportunities for intervening with siblings in isolation from their families seem limited and of uncertain benefit. Measures such as respite for the whole family as indicated above might both reach siblings more directly and be of greater therapeutic value.

Siblings' exposure to drugs and what might be done to help prevent initiation

In this study the siblings of a problem drug-using brother or sister were at elevated risk of similarly developing problems with drugs. Most siblings had been exposed to drug use in some measure, had seen drugs as well as the associated paraphernalia of needles or foil and in many cases had seen their brother or sister in the process of using drugs. However, these data indicate a complex picture. Despite the levels of exposure, deliberate and routine, reported across the sample, it did not necessarily result in drug initiation. For some siblings such exposure was a deterrent, for others it excited curiosity or legitimated experimentation, whether with the sibling or with peers.

- Although a complex picture the rates of drug exposure and initiation reported by these siblings do suggest a particular vulnerability to drug involvement that might merit the instigation of preventative work with siblings. Again this is an area where the use of mentors might hold particular promise.

The near universal view among the drug-using family members was that close proximity to the negative effects of their drug problem was a deterrent for their brothers and sisters. They did not for the most part appear to see the contrary possibility that they might model drug initiation. It is possible that problem drug users could be made aware of the dangers of exposing their family members to their drug problem and tutored as to the risks they pose. Again, however, this raises the question as to who might be best placed to deliver such a message. Currently the emphasis in treatment services is on how problem drug use impacts on the person with the problem. The ways in which it impacts on others are much less of a focus. Practitioners are largely in contact with the drug user alone and in their orientation towards them as individuals may not feel qualified or see it as appropriate to encourage them to be mindful of their potential role in drug initiation.

- Agencies charged with working with problem drug users should be encouraged to develop a more encompassing model of problem drug use and its impacts on family members. The provision of training on the impact of drugs on the wider family could facilitate a greater awareness of the potential risks to family members through being exposed to drug use. In particular attention should be drawn to the potential modelling effects of using drugs in close proximity to their siblings.

Other factors such as family background, connectedness or not to the family and involvement in conventional activities with non-deviant peers must have an important part to play in the process by which one sibling but not another, even within the same family, becomes drawn into the problematic use of drugs. One possible factor identified in this research related to the specific family dynamics created by the development of a drug problem by a close family member. With the concentration of parental attention on the drug-using child, the other children in the family would inevitably be less of a focus. Some siblings welcomed this and some did not; however, one result was a lesser ability of the parents to monitor and supervise their other children, as well as just being there for them, which could lead to problems both in terms of resentment and feeling disconnected from the family and the unchecked development of friendships that might have a detrimental influence on their behaviour.

Again it is hard to be prescriptive about what might help families to strike more of a balance between trying to address the child's drug problem and also keeping an eye on what else is happening in the family. One should certainly not underestimate the difficulties of trying to retain an even focus on all the children given the often acute, unpredictable and overwhelming torrent of problems associated with the drug use.

- A particularly valuable dimension of the work of family support groups would seem to lie in helping parents both to recognise the degree to which drugs have consumed their time and attention and to refocus on the needs of their other children.

The task of this report has been to highlight some of the difficulties confronted by families where sons or daughters, brothers or sisters develop problems with drugs. It would certainly have been much neater to conclude with concrete suggestions for intervention. However, an examination of the situations faced by families living with a family member with a drug problem suggests that there is no simple or obvious way forward. The severity and intractability of the effects on the family, coupled with the tendency for families to frame their concerns in terms of the drug-affected family member rather than the impacts on themselves, make it difficult to reach and engage families effectively. And yet it is to this challenge that we must respond with both compassion and imagination.

Notes

Chapter 1

1 The study had the full ethical approval of the University of Glasgow ethics committee.

Chapter 5

1 In all, ten telephone interviews were carried out with two members of each of the professional groups cited.

References

Bluebond-Langner, M. (1996) *In the Shadow of Illness: Parents and Siblings of the Chronically Ill Child*. Princeton, NJ: Princeton University Press

Boyd, C. and Guthrie, B. (1996) 'Women, their significant others, and crack cocaine', *The American Journal of Addiction Psychiatry*, Vol. 5, No. 2, pp. 156–66

Brook, J., Whiteman, M., Gordon, A. and Brenden, C. (1983) 'Older brother's influence on younger sibling's drug use', *Journal of Psychology*, Vol. 114, No. 1, pp. 83–90

Brook, J., Whiteman, M., Gordon, A. and Brook, D.W. (1989) 'The role of older brothers in younger brothers' drug use viewed in the context of parent and peer influences', *The Journal of Genetic Psychology*, Vol. 151, No. 1, pp. 59–75

Copello, A. and Orford, J. (2002) 'Addiction and the family: is it time for services to take notice of the evidence?', *Addiction*, Vol. 97, No. 11, pp. 1361–3

Duncan, T., Duncan, S. and Hops, H. (1996) 'The role of parents and older siblings in predicting adolescent substance use: modeling development via structural equation latent growth methodology', *Journal of Family Psychology*, Vol. 10, No. 2, pp. 158–72

EIU (Effective Interventions Unit) (2002) *Supporting Families and Carers of Drug Users: A Review*. Edinburgh: Effective Interventions Unit, Scottish Executive

Farrington, D. and Painter, K. (2004) 'Gender differences in risk factors for offending', *RDS Findings*, No. 196. London: Home Office

Gerace, L.M. (1993) 'Sibling perspectives on schizophrenia and the family', *Schizophrenia Bulletin*, Vol. 19, No. 3, pp. 637–47

Hammersley, R., Ditton, J. and Main, D. (1997) 'Drug use and sources of drug information in a 12–16-year-old school sample', *Drugs: Education, Prevention and Policy*, Vol. 4, No. 3, pp. 231–41

Huberty, D. and Huberty, C. (1986) 'Sabotaging siblings: an overlooked aspect of family therapy with drug dependent adolescents', *Journal of Psychoactive Drugs*, Vol. 18, No. 1, pp. 31–41

Jones, M. and Jones, D. (2000) 'The contagious nature of antisocial behavior', *Criminology*, Vol. 38, No. 1, pp. 25–47

Lamorey, S. (1999) 'Parentification of siblings of children with disability or chronic disease', in N.D. Chase (ed.) *Burdened Children: Theory, Research and Treatment of Parentification*. Thousand Oaks, CA: Sage Publications

Luthar, S., Merikangas, K. and Rounsaville, B. (1993) 'Parental psychopathology and disorders in offspring – a study of relatives of drug users', *The Journal of Nervous and Mental Disease*, Vol. 181, No. 6, pp. 351–7

Marcenko, M.O., Kemp, S. and Larson, N.C. (2000) 'Childhood experiences of abuse, later substance abuse and parenting outcomes among low-income mothers', *American Journal of Orthopsychiatry*, Vol. 70, No. 3, pp. 316–26

Neale, J. (2002) *Drug Users in Society.* Basingstoke: Palgrave

Needle, R., McCubbin, H., Wilson, M., Reineck, R., Lazar, A. and Mederer, H. (1986) 'Interpersonal influences in adolescent drug use – the role of older siblings, parents, and peers', *The International Journal of the Addictions,* Vol. 21, No. 7, pp. 739–66

Orford, J., Natera, G., Davies, J., Nava, A., Mora, J., Rigby, K., Bradbury, D., Copello, A. and Velleman, R. (1998) 'Tolerate, engage or withdraw: a study of the structure of families coping with alcohol and drug problems at home: findings from Mexican and English families', *Addiction,* Vol. 93, No. 12, pp. 1799–1813

Vakalahi, H. (2001) 'Adolescent substance use and family-based risk and protective factors: a literature review', *Journal of Drug Education,* Vol. 31, No. 1, pp. 29–46

Velleman, R., Bennett, G., Miller, T., Orford, J. and Tod, A. (1993) 'The families of problem drug users: a study of 50 close relatives', *Addiction,* Vol. 88, No. 9, pp. 1281–9